God's Wisdom for Fathers
is a special guide for

_____

May you find happiness as you seek
God's wisdom in leading your family.

God's *for* Wisdom FATHERS

compiled by

Jack Countryman

Thomas Nelson
Since 1798

NASHVILLE DALLAS MEXICO CITY RIO DE JANEIRO BEIJING

God's
for Wisdom
FATHERS

Published in Nashville, Tennessee, by Thomas Nelson. Thomas Nelson is a trademark of Thomas Nelson, Inc.

Thomas Nelson, Inc. titles may be purchased in bulk for educational, business, fundraising, or sales promotional use. For information, please email NelsonMinistryServices@ThomasNelson.com.

All Scripture references are from THE NEW KING JAMES VERSION® (NKJV) © 1982 Thomas Nelson, Inc. Used by permission. All rights reserved.

Cover and interior designed by Kristy Morell, Smyrna, Tennessee.

ISBN-13: 978-1-4041-1388-6

Printed in the United States of America

Contents

Preface

The Bible clearly states that "the word of God is living and powerful and sharper than any two-edged sword" (Hebrews 4:12a). This book has been created for fathers to seek God's wisdom through His Word as they cope with the many responsibilities that face men and fathers in today's culture. May this book be a guide for your life and a blessing to you personally.

God's Wisdom Is
Primary in a Father's Life

Wisdom Belongs to God

"The LORD possessed me at the beginning
   of His way,
Before His works of old.
I have been established from everlasting,
From the beginning, before there was ever an earth.
When there were no depths I was brought forth,
When there were no fountains abounding
   with water.
Before the mountains were settled,
Before the hills, I was brought forth;
While as yet He had not made the earth or
   the fields,
Or the primal dust of the world.
When He prepared the heavens, I was there,
When He drew a circle on the face of the deep,
When He established the clouds above,
When He strengthened the fountains of the deep,
When He assigned to the sea its limit,
So that the waters would not transgress His command,
When He marked out the foundations of the earth,
Then I was beside Him as a master craftsman;
And I was daily His delight,
Rejoicing always before Him,
Rejoicing in His inhabited world,
And my delight was with the sons of men."

—*Proverbs 8:22–31*

The LORD by wisdom founded the earth;
By understanding He established the heavens;
By His knowledge the depths were broken up,
And clouds drop down the dew.

—Proverbs 3:19–20

"The fear of the LORD is the beginning of wisdom,
And the knowledge of the Holy One is
    understanding.
For by me your days will be multiplied,
And years of life will be added to you."

—Proverbs 9:10–11

The preparations of the heart belong to man,
But the answer of the tongue is from the LORD.
All the ways of a man are pure in his own eyes,
But the LORD weighs the spirits.
Commit your works to the LORD,
And your thoughts will be established.

—Proverbs 16:1–3

If any of you lacks wisdom, let him ask of God,
who gives to all liberally and without reproach, and
it will be given to him.

—James 1:5

God is wise in heart and mighty in strength.
Who has hardened himself against Him
and prospered?
He removes the mountains, and they do not know
When He overturns them in His anger;
He shakes the earth out of its place,
And its pillars tremble;
He commands the sun, and it does not rise;
He seals off the stars;
He alone spreads out the heavens,
And treads on the waves of the sea;
He made the Bear, Orion, and the Pleiades,
And the chambers of the south;
He does great things past finding out,
Yes, wonders without number.

—Job 9:4–10

GOD'S WISDOM IS PRIMARY IN A FATHER'S LIFE
Seek Wisdom

My son, if you receive my words,
And treasure my commands within you,

So that you incline your ear to wisdom,
And apply your heart to understanding;
Yes, if you cry out for discernment,
And lift up your voice for understanding,
If you seek her as silver,
And search for her as for hidden treasures;
Then you will understand the fear of the LORD,
And find the knowledge of God.
For the LORD gives wisdom;
From His mouth come knowledge and
    understanding.

—Proverbs 2:1–6

Get wisdom! Get understanding!
Do not forget, nor turn away from the words
    of my mouth.
Do not forsake her, and she will preserve you;
Love her, and she will keep you.
Wisdom is the principal thing;
Therefore get wisdom.
And in all your getting, get understanding.
Exalt her, and she will promote you;

She will bring you honor, when you embrace her.
She will place on your head an ornament of grace;
A crown of glory she will deliver to you.

—Proverbs 4:5–9

Does not wisdom cry out,
And understanding lift up her voice?
She takes her stand on the top of the high hill,
Beside the way, where the paths meet.
She cries out by the gates, at the entry of the city,
At the entrance of the doors:
  "To you, O men, I call,
And my voice is to the sons of men.
O you simple ones, understand prudence,
And you fools, be of an understanding heart.
Listen, for I will speak of excellent things,
And from the opening of my lips will come
    right things;
For my mouth will speak truth;
Wickedness is an abomination to my lips.
All the words of my mouth are with righteousness;
Nothing crooked or perverse is in them.
They are all plain to him who understands,
And right to those who find knowledge.
Receive my instruction, and not silver,
And knowledge rather than choice gold;
For wisdom is better than rubies,

And all the things one may desire cannot be
    compared with her."

—Proverbs 8:1–11

Wisdom has built her house,
She has hewn out her seven pillars;
She has slaughtered her meat,
She has mixed her wine,
She has also furnished her table.
She has sent out her maidens,
She cries out from the highest places of the city,
"Whoever is simple, let him turn in here!"
As for him who lacks understanding, she says
    to him,
"Come, eat of my bread
And drink of the wine I have mixed.
Forsake foolishness and live,
And go in the way of understanding."

—Proverbs 9:1–6

He who gets wisdom loves his own soul;
He who keeps understanding will find good.

—Proverbs 19:8

Wisdom Is Valuable

Receive my instruction, and not silver,
And knowledge rather than choice gold;
For wisdom is better than rubies,
And all the things one may desire cannot be
    compared with her.

—Proverbs 8:10–11

Happy is the man who finds wisdom,
And the man who gains understanding;
For her proceeds are better than the profits
    of silver,
And her gain than fine gold.
She is more precious than rubies,
And all the things you may desire cannot
    compare with her.
Length of days is in her right hand,
In her left hand riches and honor.
Her ways are ways of pleasantness,
And all her paths are peace.
She is a tree of life to those who take hold of her,
And happy are all who retain her.

—Proverbs 3:13–18

My son, eat honey because it is good,
And the honeycomb which is sweet to your taste;
So shall the knowledge of wisdom be to your soul;
If you have found it, there is a prospect,
And your hope will not be cut off.

—Proverbs 24:13–14

The words of the wise are like goads, and the words of scholars are like well-driven nails, given by one Shepherd. And further, my son, be admonished by these. Of making many books there is no end, and much study is wearisome to the flesh.

Let us hear the conclusion of the whole matter:

Fear God and keep His commandments,
For this is man's all.
For God will bring every work into judgment,
Including every secret thing,
Whether good or evil.

—Ecclesiastes 12:11–14

Walk prudently when you go to the house of God; and draw near to hear rather than to give the sacrifice of fools, for they do not know that they do evil. Do not be rash with your mouth,
And let not your heart utter anything hastily
   before God.
For God is in heaven, and you on earth;
Therefore let your words be few.

For a dream comes through much activity,
And a fool's voice is known by his many words.
When you make a vow to God, do not delay
    to pay it;
For He has no pleasure in fools.
Pay what you have vowed—
Better not to vow than to vow and not pay.

Do not let your mouth cause your flesh to sin, nor say before the messenger of God that it was an error. Why should God be angry at your excuse and destroy the work of your hands? For in the multitude of dreams and many words there is also vanity. But fear God.

—*Ecclesiastes 5:1–7*

GOD'S WISDOM IS PRIMARY IN A FATHER'S LIFE
The Characteristics of Wisdom

"I, wisdom, dwell with prudence,
And find out knowledge and discretion.
The fear of the LORD is to hate evil;
Pride and arrogance and the evil way
And the perverse mouth I hate.
Counsel is mine, and sound wisdom;
I am understanding, I have strength."

—Proverbs 8:12–14

The words of a man's mouth are deep waters;
The wellspring of wisdom is a flowing brook.

—Proverbs 18:4

Listen, for I will speak of excellent things,
And from the opening of my lips will come
    right things;
For my mouth will speak truth;
Wickedness is an abomination to my lips.
All the words of my mouth are with righteousness;
Nothing crooked or perverse is in them.
They are all plain to him who understands,
And right to those who find knowledge.

—Proverbs 8:6–9

A soft answer turns away wrath,
But a harsh word stirs up anger.
The tongue of the wise uses knowledge rightly,
But the mouth of fools pours forth foolishness.
The eyes of the LORD are in every place,
Keeping watch on the evil and the good.
A wholesome tongue is a tree of life,
But perverseness in it breaks the spirit.
A fool despises his father's instruction,
But he who receives correction is prudent.

—Proverbs 15:1–5

A wise son heeds his father's instruction,
But a scoffer does not listen to rebuke.
A man shall eat well by the fruit of his mouth,
But the soul of the unfaithful feeds on violence.
He who guards his mouth preserves his life,
But he who opens wide his lips shall have
    destruction.
The soul of a lazy man desires, and has nothing;
But the soul of the diligent shall be made rich.
A righteous man hates lying,
But a wicked man is loathsome and comes to
shame.

—Proverbs 13:1–5

Wisdom Pays Dividends

Turn at my rebuke;
Surely I will pour out my spirit on you;
I will make my words known to you.

—Proverbs 1:23

"Now therefore, listen to me, my children,
For blessed are those who keep my ways.
Hear instruction and be wise,
And do not disdain it.
Blessed is the man who listens to me,
Watching daily at my gates,
Waiting at the posts of my doors.
For whoever finds me finds life,
And obtains favor from the LORD;
But he who sins against me wrongs his own soul;
All those who hate me love death."

—Proverbs 8:32–36

He who gets wisdom loves his own soul;
He who keeps understanding will find good.

—Proverbs 19:8

When wisdom enters your heart,
And knowledge is pleasant to your soul,
Discretion will preserve you;
Understanding will keep you,
To deliver you from the way of evil,
From the man who speaks perverse things,
From those who leave the paths of uprightness
To walk in the ways of darkness;
Who rejoice in doing evil,
And delight in the perversity of the wicked;
Whose ways are crooked,
And who are devious in their paths;
To deliver you from the immoral woman,
From the seductress who flatters with her words,
Who forsakes the companion of her youth,
And forgets the covenant of her God.
For her house leads down to death,
And her paths to the dead;
None who go to her return,
Nor do they regain the paths of life—
So you may walk in the way of goodness,
And keep to the paths of righteousness.
For the upright will dwell in the land,
And the blameless will remain in it;
But the wicked will be cut off from the earth,
And the unfaithful will be uprooted from it.

—*Proverbs 2:10–22*

My son, let them not depart from your eyes—
Keep sound wisdom and discretion;
So they will be life to your soul
And grace to your neck.
Then you will walk safely in your way,
And your foot will not stumble.
When you lie down, you will not be afraid;
Yes, you will lie down and your sleep will be sweet.
Do not be afraid of sudden terror,
Nor of trouble from the wicked when it comes;
For the LORD will be your confidence,
And will keep your foot from being caught.

—Proverbs 3:21–26

I love those who love me,
And those who seek me diligently will find me.
Riches and honor are with me,
Enduring riches and righteousness.
My fruit is better than gold, yes, than fine gold,
And my revenue than choice silver.
I traverse the way of righteousness,
In the midst of the paths of justice,
That I may cause those who love me to inherit
    wealth,
That I may fill their treasuries.

—Proverbs 8:17–21

Hear, my son, and receive my sayings,
And the years of your life will be many.
I have taught you in the way of wisdom;
I have led you in right paths.
When you walk, your steps will not be hindered,
And when you run, you will not stumble.
Take firm hold of instruction, do not let go;
Keep her, for she is your life.

—*Proverbs 4:10–13*

GOD'S WISDOM IS PRIMARY IN A FATHER'S LIFE
Do Not Reject Wisdom

Because I have called and you refused,
I have stretched out my hand and no one regarded,
Because you disdained all my counsel,
And would have none of my rebuke,
I also will laugh at your calamity;
I will mock when your terror comes,
When your terror comes like a storm,
And your destruction comes like a whirlwind,
When distress and anguish come upon you.
"Then they will call on me, but I will not answer;
They will seek me diligently, but they will not
    find me.
Because they hated knowledge
And did not choose the fear of the LORD,
They would have none of my counsel
And despised my every rebuke.
Therefore they shall eat the fruit of their own way,
And be filled to the full with their own fancies.
For the turning away of the simple will slay them,
And the complacency of fools will destroy them;
But whoever listens to me will dwell safely,
And will be secure, without fear of evil."

—*Proverbs 1:24–33*

"He who hears you hears Me, he who rejects you rejects Me, and he who rejects Me rejects Him who sent Me."

—*Luke 10:16*

For God did not call us to uncleanness, but in holiness. Therefore he who rejects this does not reject man, but God, who has also given us His Holy Spirit.

—*1 Thessalonians 4:7–8*

God's Wisdom
for Fathers Is . . .

GOD'S WISDOM FOR FATHERS IS . . .
To Worship God

"And you shall remember the LORD your God, for it is He who gives you power to get wealth, that He may establish His covenant which He swore to your fathers, as it is this day. Then it shall be, if you by any means forget the LORD your God, and follow other gods, and serve them and worship them, I testify against you this day that you shall surely perish."

—*Deuteronomy 8:18–19*

For the LORD is the great God,
And the great King above all gods.
In His hand are the deep places of the earth;
The heights of the hills are His also.
The sea is His, for He made it;
And His hands formed the dry land.
Oh come, let us worship and bow down;
Let us kneel before the Lord our Maker.
For He is our God,
And we are the people of His pasture,
And the sheep of His hand.

—*Psalm 95:3–7*

For the LORD is great and greatly to be praised;
He is to be feared above all gods. . . .
Give to the LORD the glory due His name;
Bring an offering, and come into His courts.
Oh, worship the LORD in the beauty of holiness!
Tremble before Him, all the earth.

—*Psalm 96:4, 8–9*

. . . looking unto Jesus, the author and finisher of our faith, who for the joy that was set before Him endured the cross, despising the shame, and has sat down at the right hand of the throne of God.

For consider Him who endured such hostility from sinners against Himself, lest you become weary and discouraged in your souls.

—*Hebrews 12:2–3*

Exalt the LORD our God,
And worship at His footstool—
He is holy. . . .
Exalt the LORD our God,
And worship at His holy hill;
For the LORD our God is holy.

—*Psalm 99:5, 9*

Now I, John, saw and heard these things. And when I heard and saw, I fell down to worship before the feet of the angel who showed me these things. Then he said to me, "See that you do not do that. For I am your fellow servant, and of your brethren the prophets, and of those who keep the words of this book. Worship God."

—Revelation 22:8–9

Then I saw another angel flying in the midst of heaven saying with a loud voice, "Fear God and give glory to Him, for the hour of His judgment has come; and worship Him who made heaven and earth, the sea and springs of water."

—Revelation 14:6–7

GOD'S WISDOM FOR FATHERS IS . . .
To Obey God's Word

But from there you will seek the LORD your God, and you will find Him if you seek Him with all your heart and with all your soul. When you are in distress, and all these things come upon you in the latter days, when you turn to the LORD your God and obey His voice (for the LORD your God is a merciful God), He will not forsake you nor destroy you, nor forget the covenant of your fathers which He swore to them.

—Deuteronomy 4:29–31

But Jesus answered him, saying, "It is written, 'Man shall not live by bread alone, but by every word of God.'"

—Luke 4:4

As for God, His way is perfect;
The word of the LORD is proven;
He is a shield to all who trust in Him.

—Psalm 18:30

For the word of God is living and powerful, and sharper than any two-edged sword, piercing even to

the division of soul and spirit, and of joints and marrow, and is a discerner of the thoughts and intents
of the heart.

—*Hebrews 4:12*

The law of the LORD is perfect, converting the soul;
The testimony of the LORD is sure, making wise
    the simple;
The statutes of the LORD are right, rejoicing
    the heart;
The commandment of the LORD is pure,
    enlightening the eyes.

—*Psalm 19:7–8*

    Draw near to God and He will draw near to you.
Cleanse your hands, you sinners; and purify your
hearts, you double-minded.

—*James 4:8*

As for God, His way is perfect;
The word of the LORD is proven;
He is a shield to all who trust in Him.

—*Psalm 18:30*

To Come to God in Prayer

"Ask, and it will be given to you; seek, and you will find; knock, and it will be opened to you. For everyone who asks receives, and he who seeks finds, and to him who knocks it will be opened."

—Matthew 7:7–8

Be anxious for nothing, but in everything by prayer and supplication, with thanksgiving, let your requests be made known to God; and the peace of God, which surpasses all understanding, will guard your hearts and minds through Christ Jesus.

—Philippians 4:6–7

"Call to Me, and I will answer you, and show you great and mighty things, which you do not know."

—Jeremiah 33:3

If My people who are called by My name will humble themselves, and pray and seek My face, and turn from their wicked ways, then I will hear from heaven, and will forgive their sin and heal their land.

—2 Chronicles 7:14

And take . . . the sword of the Spirit, which is the word of God; praying always with all prayer and supplication in the Spirit, being watchful to this end with all perseverance and supplication for all the saints.

—Ephesians 6:17–18

Hear me when I call, O God of my righteousness!
You have relieved me in my distress;
Have mercy on me, and hear my prayer.

—Psalm 4:1

Rejoice always, pray without ceasing, in everything give thanks; for this is the will of God in Christ Jesus for you.

—1 Thessalonians 5:16–18

GOD'S WISDOM FOR FATHERS IS . . .

To Listen to the Holy Spirit

His divine power has given to us all things that pertain to life and godliness, through the knowledge of Him who called us by glory and virtue, by which have been given to us exceedingly great and precious promises, that through these you may be partakers of the divine nature, having escaped the corruption that is in the world through lust.

—2 Peter 1:3–4

But the fruit of the Spirit is love, joy, peace, long-suffering, kindness, goodness, faithfulness, gentleness, self-control. Against such there is no law. And those who are Christ's have crucified the flesh with its passions and desires. If we live in the Spirit, let us also walk in the Spirit.

—Galatians 5:22–25

"If you ask anything in My name, I will do it. If you love Me, keep My commandments. And I will pray the Father, and He will give you another Helper, that He may abide with you forever—the Spirit of truth, whom the world cannot receive, because it neither sees Him nor knows Him; but you know Him, for He dwells with you and will be in you. I will

~27~

not leave you orphans; I will come to you . . . But the Helper, the Holy Spirit, whom the Father will send in My name, He will teach you all things, and bring to your remembrance all things that I said to you."

—John 14:14–18, 26

"Nevertheless I tell you the truth. It is to your advantage that I go away; for if I do not go away, the Helper will not come to you; but if I depart, I will send Him to you. . . .

"However, when He, the Spirit of truth, has come, He will guide you into all truth; for He will not speak on His own authority, but whatever He hears He will speak; and He will tell you things to come."

—John 16:7, 13

"For everyone who asks receives, and he who seeks finds, and to him who knocks it will be opened.

"If a son asks for bread from any father among you, will he give him a stone? Or if he asks for a fish, will he give him a serpent instead of a fish? Or if he asks for an egg, will he offer him a scorpion? If you then, being evil, know how to give good gifts to your children, how much more will your heavenly Father give the Holy Spirit to those who ask Him!"

—Luke 11:10–13

But as it is written:
"Eye has not seen, nor ear heard,
Nor have entered into the heart of man
The things which God has prepared for those
    who love Him."
But God has revealed them to us through His Spirit. For the Spirit searches all things, yes, the deep things of God. For what man knows the things of a man except the spirit of the man which is in him? Even so no one knows the things of God except the Spirit of God. Now we have received, not the spirit of the world, but the Spirit who is from God, that we might know the things that have been freely given to us by God. These things we also speak, not in words which man's wisdom teaches but which the Holy Spirit teaches, comparing spiritual things with spiritual. But the natural man does not receive the things of the Spirit of God, for they are foolishness to him; nor can he know them, because they are spiritually discerned.

—*1 Corinthians 2:9–14*

[God has] made us sufficient as ministers of the new covenant, not of the letter but of the Spirit; for the letter kills, but the Spirit gives life. . . .

Now the Lord is the Spirit; and where the Spirit of the Lord is, there is liberty. But we all, with unveiled face, beholding as in a mirror the glory of the Lord, are being transformed into the same image from glory to glory, just as by the Spirit of the Lord.

—2 Corinthians 3:6, 17–18

But if the Spirit of Him who raised Jesus from the dead dwells in you, He who raised Christ from the dead will also give life to your mortal bodies through His Spirit who dwells in you. . . .

The Spirit Himself bears witness with our spirit that we are children of God, and if children, then heirs—heirs of God and joint heirs with Christ, if indeed we suffer with Him, that we may also be glorified together.

For I consider that the sufferings of this present time are not worthy to be compared with the glory which shall be revealed in us. . . .

Likewise the Spirit also helps in our weaknesses. For we do not know what we should pray for as we ought, but the Spirit Himself makes intercession for us with groanings which cannot be uttered. Now He who searches the hearts knows what the mind of the Spirit is, because He makes intercession for the saints according to the will of God.

—Romans 8:11, 16–18, 26–27

God's Promises
for Fathers

Eternal Life

And as Moses lifted up the serpent in the wilderness, even so must the Son of Man be lifted up, that whoever believes in Him should not perish but have eternal life. For God so loved the world that He gave His only begotten Son, that whoever believes in Him should not perish but have everlasting life. For God did not send His Son into the world to condemn the world, but that the world through Him might be saved.

—John 3:14–17

Therefore let that abide in you which you heard from the beginning. If what you heard from the beginning abides in you, you also will abide in the Son and in the Father. And this is the promise that He has promised us—eternal life.

—1 John 2:24–25

But we see Jesus, who was made a little lower than the angels, for the suffering of death crowned with glory and honor, that He, by the grace of God, might taste death for everyone.

For it was fitting for Him, for whom are all things and by whom are all things, in bringing many sons

to glory, to make the captain of their salvation perfect through sufferings. For both He who sanctifies and those who are being sanctified are all of one, for which reason He is not ashamed to call them brethren, saying:
"I will declare Your name to My brethren;
In the midst of the assembly I will sing praise
  to You."
And again:
"I will put My trust in Him."
And again:
"Here am I and the children whom God has given Me."

Inasmuch then as the children have partaken of flesh and blood, He Himself likewise shared in the same, that through death He might destroy him who had the power of death, that is, the devil, and release those who through fear of death were all their lifetime subject to bondage.

—Hebrews 2:9–15

Behold, I tell you a mystery: We shall not all sleep, but we shall all be changed—in a moment, in the twinkling of an eye, at the last trumpet. For the trumpet will sound, and the dead will be raised incorruptible, and we shall be changed. For this corruptible must put on incorruption, and this mortal must put on immortality. So when this corruptible has put on incorruption, and this mortal has put on immortality, then shall be brought to pass the saying that is written: "Death is swallowed up in victory. O Death, where is your sting? O Hades, where is your victory?"

The sting of death is sin, and the strength of sin is the law. But thanks be to God, who gives us the victory through our Lord Jesus Christ.

—*1 Corinthians 15:51–57*

Who is he who condemns? It is Christ who died, and furthermore is also risen, who is even at the right hand of God, who also makes intercession for us. Who shall separate us from the love of Christ? Shall tribulation, or distress, or persecution, or famine, or nakedness, or peril, or sword? As it is written:

"For Your sake we are killed all day long;
We are accounted as sheep for the slaughter."

Yet in all these things we are more than conquerors through Him who loved us. For I am persuaded that neither death nor life, nor angels nor principalities nor powers, nor things present nor things to come, nor height nor depth, nor any other created thing, shall be able to separate us from the love of God which is in Christ Jesus our Lord.

—*Romans 8:34–39*

"The thief does not come except to steal, and to kill, and to destroy. I have come that they may have life, and that they may have it more abundantly....

"My sheep hear My voice, and I know them, and they follow Me. And I give them eternal life, and they shall never perish; neither shall anyone snatch them out of My hand. My Father, who has given them to Me, is greater than all; and no one is able to snatch them out of My Father's hand. I and My Father are one."

—*John 10:10, 27–30*

He will swallow up death forever,
And the Lord GOD will wipe away tears from
    all faces;
The rebuke of His people
He will take away from all the earth;
For the LORD has spoken.
And it will be said in that day:
"Behold, this is our God;
We have waited for Him, and He will save us.
This is the LORD;
We have waited for Him;
We will be glad and rejoice in His salvation."

—*Isaiah 25:8–9*

Safety

Blessed is the nation whose God is the LORD,
The people He has chosen as His own inheritance.
The LORD looks from heaven;
He sees all the sons of men.
From the place of His dwelling He looks
On all the inhabitants of the earth;
He fashions their hearts individually;
He considers all their works.
No king is saved by the multitude of an army;
A mighty man is not delivered by great strength.
A horse is a vain hope for safety;
Neither shall it deliver any by its great strength.
Behold, the eye of the LORD is on those who fear Him,
On those who hope in His mercy,
To deliver their soul from death,
And to keep them alive in famine.
Our soul waits for the LORD;
He is our help and our shield.

—*Psalm 33:12–20*

The LORD also will be a refuge for the oppressed,
A refuge in times of trouble.
And those who know Your name will put their
    trust in You;

For You, LORD, have not forsaken those who
  seek You.
Sing praises to the LORD, who dwells in Zion!
Declare His deeds among the people.
When He avenges blood, He remembers them;
He does not forget the cry of the humble.

—*Psalm 9:9–12*

Therefore humble yourselves under the mighty
hand of God, that He may exalt you in due time,
casting all your care upon Him, for He cares for you.
Be sober, be vigilant; because your adversary the
devil walks about like a roaring lion, seeking whom
he may devour. Resist him, steadfast in the faith,
knowing that the same sufferings are experienced by
your brotherhood in the world. But may the God of
all grace, who called us to His eternal glory by Christ
Jesus, after you have suffered a while, perfect, establish, strengthen, and settle you. To Him be the glory
and the dominion forever and ever. Amen.

—*1 Peter 5:7–11*

I will lift up my eyes to the hills—
From whence comes my help?
My help comes from the LORD,
Who made heaven and earth.
He will not allow your foot to be moved;

He who keeps you will not slumber.
Behold, He who keeps Israel
Shall neither slumber nor sleep.
The LORD is your keeper;
The LORD is your shade at your right hand.
The sun shall not strike you by day,
Nor the moon by night.
The LORD shall preserve you from all evil;
He shall preserve your soul.
The LORD shall preserve your going out and
    your coming in
From this time forth, and even forevermore.
—Psalm 121:1–8

Make haste, O God, to deliver me!
Make haste to help me, O LORD!
Let them be ashamed and confounded
Who seek my life;
Let them be turned back and confused
Who desire my hurt.
Let them be turned back because of their shame,
Who say, "Aha, aha!"
Let all those who seek You rejoice and be glad
    in You;
And let those who love Your salvation say
    continually,
"Let God be magnified!"
But I am poor and needy;

Make haste to me, O God!
You are my help and my deliverer;
O LORD, do not delay.

—Psalm 70:1–5

In You, O Lord, I put my trust;
Let me never be put to shame.
Deliver me in Your righteousness, and cause me
    to escape;
Incline Your ear to me, and save me.
Be my strong refuge,
To which I may resort continually;
You have given the commandment to save me,
For You are my rock and my fortress.
Deliver me, O my God, out of the hand of
    the wicked,
Out of the hand of the unrighteous and cruel man.
For You are my hope, O Lord GOD;
You are my trust from my youth.
By You I have been upheld from birth;
You are He who took me out of my
    mother's womb.
My praise shall be continually of You.
I have become as a wonder to many,
But You are my strong refuge.

—Psalm 71:1–7

Peace

Open the gates,
That the righteous nation which keeps the truth
    may enter in.
You will keep him in perfect peace,
Whose mind is stayed on You,
Because he trusts in You.
Trust in the LORD forever,
For in YAH, the LORD, is everlasting strength
                       —*Isaiah 26:2–4*

"Peace I leave with you, My peace I give to you; not as the world gives do I give to you. Let not your heart be troubled, neither let it be afraid."
                       —*John 14:27*

"These things I have spoken to you, that in Me you may have peace. In the world you will have tribulation; but be of good cheer, I have overcome the world."
                       —*John 16:33*

Pray for the peace of Jerusalem:
"May they prosper who love you.
Peace be within your walls,

Prosperity within your palaces."
For the sake of my brethren and companions,
I will now say, "Peace be within you."
Because of the house of the LORD our God
I will seek your good.

—*Psalm 122:6–9*

I rejoice at Your word
As one who finds great treasure.
I hate and abhor lying,
But I love Your law.
Seven times a day I praise You,
Because of Your righteous judgments.
Great peace have those who love Your law,
And nothing causes them to stumble.

—*Psalm 119:162–165*

Therefore, having been justified by faith, we have peace with God through our Lord Jesus Christ, through whom also we have access by faith into this grace in which we stand, and rejoice in hope of the glory of God.

—*Romans 5:1–2*

And let the peace of God rule in your hearts, to which also you were called in one body; and be thankful.

—*Colossians 3:15*

Comfort

Unless the LORD had been my help,
My soul would soon have settled in silence.
If I say, "My foot slips,"
Your mercy, O LORD, will hold me up.
In the multitude of my anxieties within me,
Your comforts delight my soul.

—*Psalm 94:17–19*

This is my comfort in my affliction,
For Your word has given me life.
The proud have me in great derision,
Yet I do not turn aside from Your law.
I remembered Your judgments of old, O LORD,
And have comforted myself.

—*Psalm 119:50–52*

"Comfort, yes, comfort My people!"
Says your God.
"Speak comfort to Jerusalem, and cry out to her,
That her warfare is ended,
That her iniquity is pardoned;
For she has received from the L LORD's hand
Double for all her sins" . . .

Every valley shall be exalted
And every mountain and hill brought low;
The crooked places shall be made straight
And the rough places smooth;
The glory of the LORD shall be revealed,
And all flesh shall see it together;
For the mouth of the LORD has spoken."

—Isaiah 40:1–2, 4–5

Blessed be the God and Father of our Lord Jesus Christ, the Father of mercies and God of all comfort, who comforts us in all our tribulation, that we may be able to comfort those who are in any trouble, with the comfort with which we ourselves are comforted by God. For as the sufferings of Christ abound in us, so our consolation also abounds through Christ. Now if we are afflicted, it is for your consolation and salvation, which is effective for enduring the same sufferings which we also suffer. Or if we are comforted, it is for your consolation and salvation. And our hope for you is steadfast, because we know that as you are partakers of the sufferings, so also you will partake of the consolation.

—2 Corinthians 1:3–7

Fear not, for I am with you;
Be not dismayed, for I am your God.

I will strengthen you,
Yes, I will help you,
I will uphold you with My righteous right hand.
—Isaiah 41:10

Power

Therefore, my beloved and longed-for brethren, my joy and crown, so stand fast in the Lord, beloved. . . .

Not that I speak in regard to need, for I have learned in whatever state I am, to be content: I know how to be abased, and I know how to abound. Everywhere and in all things I have learned both to be full and to be hungry, both to abound and to suffer need. I can do all things through Christ who strengthens me.

—*Philippians 4:1, 11–13*

Have you not known?
Have you not heard?
The everlasting God, the LORD,
The Creator of the ends of the earth,
Neither faints nor is weary.
His understanding is unsearchable.
He gives power to the weak,
And to those who have no might He increases
    strength.
Even the youths shall faint and be weary,
And the young men shall utterly fall,
But those who wait on the LORD
Shall renew their strength;
They shall mount up with wings like eagles,

They shall run and not be weary,
They shall walk and not faint.

—Isaiah 40:28–31

"Believe Me that I am in the Father and the Father in Me, or else believe Me for the sake of the works themselves. Most assuredly, I say to you, he who believes in Me, the works that I do he will do also; and greater works than these he will do, because I go to My Father. And whatever you ask in My name, that I will do, that the Father may be glorified in the Son."

—John 14:11–13

And He said to them, "It is not for you to know times or seasons which the Father has put in His own authority. But you shall receive power when the Holy Spirit has come upon you; and you shall be witnesses to Me in Jerusalem, and in all Judea and Samaria, and to the end of the earth."

—Acts 1:7–8

Concerning this thing I pleaded with the Lord three times that it might depart from me. And He said to me, "My grace is sufficient for you, for My strength is made perfect in weakness." Therefore most gladly I will rather boast in my infirmities, that the power of Christ may rest upon me. Therefore I take pleasure in infirmities, in reproaches, in needs, in persecutions, in distresses, for Christ's sake. For when I am weak, then I am strong.

—2 Corinthians 12:8–10

Therefore I ask that you do not lose heart at my tribulations for you, which is your glory.

For this reason I bow my knees to the Father of our Lord Jesus Christ, from whom the whole family in heaven and earth is named, that He would grant you, according to the riches of His glory, to be strengthened with might through His Spirit in the inner man. . . .

Now to Him who is able to do exceedingly abundantly above all that we ask or think, according to the power that works in us, to Him be glory in the church by Christ Jesus to all generations, forever and ever. Amen.

—Ephesians 3:13–16, 20–21

Justice

Do not fret because of evildoers,
Nor be envious of the workers of iniquity.
For they shall soon be cut down like the grass,
And wither as the green herb.
Trust in the LORD, and do good;
Dwell in the land, and feed on His faithfulness.

—*Psalm 37:1–3*

Arise, O LORD, in Your anger;
Lift Yourself up because of the rage of my enemies;
Rise up for me to the judgment You have
    commanded!
So the congregation of the peoples shall
    surround You;
For their sakes, therefore, return on high.
The LORD shall judge the peoples;
Judge me, O LORD, according to my righteousness,
And according to my integrity within me.
Oh, let the wickedness of the wicked come to
    an end,
But establish the just;
For the righteous God tests the hearts and minds.
My defense is of God,
Who saves the upright in heart.

God is a just judge,
And God is angry with the wicked every day.
I will praise the LORD according to His
    righteousness,
And will sing praise to the name of the LORD
    Most High.

—*Psalm 7:6–11, 17*

Vindicate me, O LORD,
For I have walked in my integrity.
I have also trusted in the Lord;
I shall not slip.
Examine me, O LORD, and prove me;
Try my mind and my heart.
For Your lovingkindness is before my eyes,
And I have walked in Your truth. . . .
I will wash my hands in innocence;
So I will go about Your altar, O LORD.

—*Psalm 26:1–3, 6*

But God is the Judge:
He puts down one,
And exalts another.
For in the hand of the LORD there is a cup,
And the wine is red;
It is fully mixed, and He pours it out;
Surely its dregs shall all the wicked of the earth

Drain and drink down.
But I will declare forever,
I will sing praises to the God of Jacob.
"All the horns of the wicked I will also cut off,
But the horns of the righteous shall be exalted."

—Psalm 75:7–10

I will praise You, O LORD, with my whole heart;
I will tell of all Your marvelous works.
I will be glad and rejoice in You;
I will sing praise to Your name, O Most High.
When my enemies turn back,
They shall fall and perish at Your presence.
For You have maintained my right and my cause;
You sat on the throne judging in righteousness.
You have rebuked the nations,
You have destroyed the wicked;
You have blotted out their name forever and ever.
O enemy, destructions are finished forever!
And you have destroyed cities;
Even their memory has perished.
But the LORD shall endure forever;
He has prepared His throne for judgment.
He shall judge the world in righteousness,
And He shall administer judgment for the
    peoples in uprightness.
The LORD also will be a refuge for the oppressed,
A refuge in times of trouble.

—Psalm 9:1–9

Moreover it is required in stewards that one be found faithful. But with me it is a very small thing that I should be judged by you or by a human court. In fact, I do not even judge myself. For I know of nothing against myself, yet I am not justified by this; but He who judges me is the Lord. Therefore judge nothing before the time, until the Lord comes, who will both bring to light the hidden things of darkness and reveal the counsels of the hearts. Then each one's praise will come from God.

—1 Corinthians 4:2–5

Wisdom

If any of you lacks wisdom, let him ask of God, who gives to all liberally and without reproach, and it will be given to him. But let him ask in faith, with no doubting, for he who doubts is like a wave of the sea driven and tossed by the wind.

—*James 1:5–6*

My son, if you receive my words,
And treasure my commands within you,
So that you incline your ear to wisdom,
And apply your heart to understanding;
Yes, if you cry out for discernment,
And lift up your voice for understanding,
If you seek her as silver,
And search for her as for hidden treasures;
Then you will understand the fear of the LORD,
And find the knowledge of God.
For the LORD gives wisdom;
From His mouth come knowledge and
    understanding;
He stores up sound wisdom for the upright;
He is a shield to those who walk uprightly.

—*Proverbs 2:1–7*

The fear of the LORD is the beginning of wisdom;
A good understanding have all those who do His
    commandments.
His praise endures forever.

—*Psalm 111:10*

For this reason we also, since the day we heard it, do not cease to pray for you, and to ask that you may be filled with the knowledge of His will in all wisdom and spiritual understanding; that you may walk worthy of the Lord, fully pleasing Him, being fruitful in every good work and increasing in the knowledge of God.

—*Colossians 1:9–10*

Let no one deceive himself. If anyone among you seems to be wise in this age, let him become a fool that he may become wise. For the wisdom of this world is foolishness with God. For it is written, "He catches the wise in their own craftiness"; and again, "The LORD knows the thoughts of the wise, that they are futile." Therefore let no one boast in men. For all things are yours.

—*1 Corinthians 3:18–21*

For you see your calling, brethren, that not many wise according to the flesh, not many mighty, not many noble, are called. But God has chosen the foolish things of the world to put to shame the wise, and God has chosen the weak things of the world to put to shame the things which are mighty; and the base things of the world and the things which are despised God has chosen, and the things which are not, to bring to nothing the things that are, that no flesh should glory in His presence. But of Him you are in Christ Jesus, who became for us wisdom from God—and righteousness and sanctification and redemption—that, as it is written, "He who glories, let him glory in the LORD."

—*1 Corinthians 1:26–31*

Forgiveness

There is therefore now no condemnation to those who are in Christ Jesus, who do not walk according to the flesh, but according to the Spirit. For the law of the Spirit of life in Christ Jesus has made me free from the law of sin and death.

—Romans 8:1–2

If we confess our sins, He is faithful and just to forgive us our sins and to cleanse us from all unrighteousness.

—1 John 1:9

. . . giving thanks to the Father who has qualified us to be partakers of the inheritance of the saints in the light. He has delivered us from the power of darkness and conveyed us into the kingdom of the Son of His love, in whom we have redemption through His blood, the forgiveness of sins.

—Colossians 1:12–14

And be kind to one another, tenderhearted, forgiving one another, even as God in Christ forgave you.

—Ephesians 4:32

"Come now, and let us reason together,"
Says the LORD,

"Though your sins are like scarlet,
They shall be as white as snow;
Though they are red like crimson,
They shall be as wool."

—*Isaiah 1:18*

"And whenever you stand praying, if you have anything against anyone, forgive him, that your Father in heaven may also forgive you your trespasses."
—*Mark 11:25*

He has not dealt with us according to our sins,
Nor punished us according to our iniquities.
For as the heavens are high above the earth,
So great is His mercy toward those who fear Him;
As far as the east is from the west,
So far has He removed our transgressions from us.
—*Psalm 103:10–12*

God's Wisdom in
Your Relationships

... *with Your Children*

Behold, children are a heritage from the LORD,
The fruit of the womb is a reward.
Like arrows in the hand of a warrior,
So are the children of one's youth.
Happy is the man who has his quiver full of them;
They shall not be ashamed,
But shall speak with their enemies in the gate.
—Psalm 127:3–5

Blessed is every one who fears the LORD,
Who walks in His ways.
When you eat the labor of your hands,
You shall be happy, and it shall be well with you.
Your wife shall be like a fruitful vine
In the very heart of your house,
Your children like olive plants
All around your table.
Behold, thus shall the man be blessed
Who fears the LORD.

—Psalm 128:1–4

The righteous man walks in his integrity;
His children are blessed after him.
—Proverbs 20:7

My son, do not despise the chastening of the LORD,
Nor detest His correction;
For whom the LORD loves He corrects,
Just as a father the son in whom he delights
—*Proverbs 3:11–12*

Therefore know this day, and consider it in your heart, that the LORD Himself is God in heaven above and on the earth beneath; there is no other. You shall therefore keep His statutes and His commandments which I command you today, that it may go well with you and with your children after you, and that you may prolong your days in the land which the LORD your God is giving you for all time.
—*Deuteronomy 4:39–40*

And you, fathers, do not provoke your children to wrath, but bring them up in the training and admonition of the Lord.

—*Ephesians 6:4*

. . . one who rules his own house well, having his children in submission with all reverence (for if a man does not know how to rule his own house, how will he take care of the church of God?).
—*1 Timothy 3:4–5*

Correct your son, and he will give you rest;
Yes, he will give delight to your soul.

—*Proverbs 29:17*

... with Your Spouse

The Pharisees also came to Him, testing Him, and saying to Him, "Is it lawful for a man to divorce his wife for just any reason?" And He answered and said to them, "Have you not read that He who made them at the beginning 'made them male and female,' and said, 'For this reason a man shall leave his father and mother and be joined to his wife, and the two shall become one flesh'? So then, they are no longer two but one flesh. Therefore what God has joined together, let not man separate." They said to Him, "Why then did Moses command to give a certificate of divorce, and to put her away?" He said to them, "Moses, because of the hardness of your hearts, permitted you to divorce your wives, but from the beginning it was not so.

—*Matthew 19:3–8*

Let the husband render to his wife the affection due her, and likewise also the wife to her husband. The wife does not have authority over her own body, but the husband does. And likewise the husband does not have authority over his own body, but the wife does. Do not deprive one another except with consent for a time, that you may give yourselves to fasting and prayer; and come together again so that Satan does not tempt you because of your lack of self-control. . . .

Now to the married I command, yet not I but the Lord: A wife is not to depart from her husband. But even if she does depart, let her remain unmarried or be reconciled to her husband. And a husband is not to divorce his wife.But to the rest I, not the Lord, say: If any brother has a wife who does not believe, and she is willing to live with him, let him not divorce her. And a woman who has a husband who does not believe, if he is willing to live with her, let her not divorce him. For the unbelieving husband is sanctified by the wife, and the unbelieving wife is sanctified by the husband; otherwise your children would be unclean, but now they are holy. But if the unbeliever departs, let him depart; a brother or a sister is not under bondage in such cases. But God has called us to peace. For how do you know, O wife, whether you will save your husband? Or how do you know, O husband, whether you will save your wife?

—*1 Corinthians 7:3–5, 10–16*

An excellent wife is the crown of her husband,
But she who causes shame is like rottenness in
   his bones.

—*Proverbs 12:4*

Marriage is honorable among all, and the bed undefiled; but fornicators and adulterers God will judge.
—*Hebrews 13:4*

. . . giving thanks always for all things to God the
Father in the name of our Lord Jesus Christ, sub-
mitting to one another in the fear of God.

Wives, submit to your own husbands, as to the
Lord. For the husband is head of the wife, as also
Christ is head of the church; and He is the Savior of
the body. Therefore, just as the church is subject to
Christ, so let the wives be to their own husbands in
everything. Husbands, love your wives, just as Christ
also loved the church and gave Himself for her, that
He might sanctify and cleanse her with the washing
of water by the word, that He might present her to
Himself a glorious church, not having spot or wrinkle
or any such thing, but that she should be holy and
without blemish. So husbands ought to love their own
wives as their own bodies; he who loves his wife loves
himself. For no one ever hated his own flesh, but
nourishes and cherishes it, just as the Lord does the
church. For we are members of His body, of His flesh
and of His bones. "For this reason a man shall leave
his father and mother and be joined to his wife, and
the two shall become one flesh." This is a great mystery, but I speak concerning Christ and the church.
Nevertheless let each one of you in particular so love

his own wife as himself, and let the wife see that she respects her husband.

—Ephesians 5:20–33

Drink water from your own cistern,
And running water from your own well.
Should your fountains be dispersed abroad,
Streams of water in the streets?
Let them be only your own,
And not for strangers with you.
Let your fountain be blessed,
And rejoice with the wife of your youth.

—Proverbs 5:15–18

GOD'S WISDOM IN YOUR RELATIONSHIPS
... *with Your Parents*

Children, obey your parents in the Lord, for this is right. "Honor your father and mother," which is the first commandment with promise: "that it may be well with you and you may live long on the earth."

—*Ephesians 6:1–3*

My son, hear the instruction of your father,
And do not forsake the law of your mother;
For they will be a graceful ornament on your head,
And chains about your neck.

—*Proverbs 1:8–9*

Children, obey your parents in all things, for this is well pleasing to the Lord.

—*Colossians 3:20*

"Honor your father and your mother, that your days may be long upon the land which the LORD your God is giving you."

—*Exodus 20:12*

The proverbs of Solomon:

A wise son makes a glad father,
But a foolish son is the grief of his mother.
—Proverbs 10:1

Listen to your father who begot you,
And do not despise your mother when she is old.
—Proverbs 23:22

Children, obey your parents in all things, for this is well pleasing to the Lord.
—Colossians 3:20

Furthermore, we have had human fathers who corrected us, and we paid them respect. Shall we not much more readily be in subjection to the Father of spirits and live?
—Hebrews 12:9

GOD'S WISDOM IN YOUR RELATIONSHIPS
... with Your Neighbors

Then one of them, a lawyer, asked Him a question, testing Him, and saying, "Teacher, which is the great commandment in the law?" Jesus said to him, 'You shall love the LORD your God with all your heart, with all your soul, and with all your mind.' This is the first and great commandment. And the second is like it: 'You shall love your neighbor as yourself.' On these two commandments hang all the Law and the Prophets."

—*Matthew 22:35–40*

And behold, a certain lawyer stood up and tested Him, saying, "Teacher, what shall I do to inherit eternal life?" He said to him, "What is written in the law? What is your reading of it?" So he answered and said, "'You shall love the LORD your God with all your heart, with all your soul, with all your strength, and with all your mind,' and 'your neighbor as yourself.'" And He said to him, "You have answered rightly; do this and you will live."

But he, wanting to justify himself, said to Jesus, "And who is my neighbor?" Then Jesus answered and said: "A certain man went down from Jerusalem to Jericho, and fell among thieves, who stripped him of his clothing, wounded him, and departed, leaving him half dead. Now by chance a certain priest came down that road. And when he saw him, he passed by on the other side. Likewise a Levite, when he arrived at the place, came and looked, and passed by on the other side. But a certain Samaritan, as he journeyed, came where he was. And when he saw him, he had compassion. So he went to him and bandaged his wounds, pouring on oil and wine; and he set him on his own animal, brought him to an inn, and took care of him. On the next day, when he departed, he took out two denarii, gave them to the innkeeper, and said to him, 'Take care of him; and whatever more you spend, when I come again, I will repay you.' So which of these three do you think was neighbor to him who fell among the thieves?" And he said, "He who showed mercy on him."

Then Jesus said to him, "Go and do likewise."

—*Luke 10:25–37*

Love does no harm to a neighbor; therefore love is the fulfillment of the law.

—*Romans 13:10*

We then who are strong ought to bear with the scruples of the weak, and not to please ourselves. Let each of us please his neighbor for his good, leading to edification. For even Christ did not please Himself; but as it is written, "The reproaches of those who reproached You fell on Me."

—Romans 15:1–3

Do not withhold good from those to whom it is due,
When it is in the power of your hand to do so.
Do not say to your neighbor,
"Go, and come back,
And tomorrow I will give it,"
When you have it with you.
Do not devise evil against your neighbor,
For he dwells by you for safety's sake.

—Proverbs 3:27–29

"You shall not covet your neighbor's house; you shall not covet your neighbor's wife, nor his male servant, nor his female servant, nor his ox, nor his donkey, nor anything that is your neighbor's."

—Exodus 20:17

Therefore, putting away lying, "Let each one of you speak truth with his neighbor," for we are members of one another.

—Ephesians 4:25

. . . *with Other Christians*

"As the Father loved Me, I also have loved you; abide in My love. If you keep My commandments, you will abide in My love, just as I have kept My Father's commandments and abide in His love. These things I have spoken to you, that My joy may remain in you, and that your joy may be full.

"This is My commandment, that you love one another as I have loved you."

—*John 15:9–12*

I, therefore, the prisoner of the Lord, beseech you to walk worthy of the calling with which you were called, with all lowliness and gentleness, with longsuffering, bearing with one another in love, endeavoring to keep the unity of the Spirit in the bond of peace. There is one body and one Spirit, just as you were called in one hope of your calling.

—*Ephesians 4:1–4*

For this reason I bow my knees to the Father of our Lord Jesus Christ, from whom the whole family in heaven and earth is named, that He would grant you, according to the riches of His glory, to be strengthened with might through His Spirit in the inner man, that Christ may dwell in your hearts through faith; that you, being rooted and grounded in love, may be able to comprehend with all the saints what is the width and length and depth and height—to know the love of Christ which passes knowledge; that you may be filled with all the fullness of God.

—*Ephesians 3:14–19*

Owe no one anything except to love one another, for he who loves another has fulfilled the law. For the commandments, "You shall not commit adultery," "You shall not murder," "You shall not steal," "You shall not bear false witness," "You shall not covet," and if there is any other commandment, are all summed up in this saying, namely, "You shall love your neighbor as yourself." Love does no harm to a neighbor; therefore love is the fulfillment of the law.

—*Romans 13:8–10*

By this we know love, because He laid down His life for us. And we also ought to lay down our lives for the brethren. But whoever has this world's goods, and sees his brother in need, and shuts up his heart from him, how does the love of God abide in him? My little children, let us not love in word or in tongue, but in deed and in truth.

—*1 John 3:16–18*

Now may the God of patience and comfort grant you to be like-minded toward one another, according to Christ Jesus, that you may with one mind and one mouth glorify the God and Father of our Lord Jesus Christ.

Therefore receive one another, just as Christ also received us, to the glory of God.

—*Romans 15:5–7*

This is the message which we have heard from Him and declare to you, that God is light and in Him is no darkness at all. If we say that we have fellowship with Him, and walk in darkness, we lie and do not practice the truth. But if we walk in the light as He is in the light, we have fellowship with one another, and the blood of Jesus Christ His Son cleanses us from all sin.

—*1 John 1:5–7*

And if Christ is in you, the body is dead because of sin, but the Spirit is life because of righteousness. But if the Spirit of Him who raised Jesus from the dead dwells in you, He who raised Christ from the dead will also give life to your mortal bodies through His Spirit who dwells in you.

Therefore, brethren, we are debtors—not to the flesh, to live according to the flesh. For if you live according to the flesh you will die; but if by the Spirit you put to death the deeds of the body, you will live. For as many as are led by the Spirit of God, these are sons of God.

—*Romans 8:10–14*

... with Strangers

"Then the King will say to those on His right hand,
'Come, you blessed of My Father, inherit the kingdom prepared for you from the foundation of the
world: for I was hungry and you gave Me food; I was
thirsty and you gave Me drink; I was a stranger and
you took Me in; I was naked and you clothed Me; I
was sick and you visited Me; I was in prison and you
came to Me.' Then the righteous will answer Him,
saying, 'Lord, when did we see You hungry and feed
You, or thirsty and give You drink? When did we
see You a stranger and take You in, or naked and
clothe You? Or when did we see You sick, or in
prison, and come to You?' And the King will answer
and say to them, 'Assuredly, I say to you, inasmuch as
you did it to one of the least of these My brethren,
you did it to Me.' Then He will also say to those on
the left hand, 'Depart from Me, you cursed, into the
everlasting fire prepared for the devil and his angels:
for I was hungry and you gave Me no food; I was
thirsty and you gave Me no drink; I was a stranger
and you did not take Me in, naked and you did not
clothe Me, sick and in prison and you did not visit
Me.' "Then they also will answer Him, saying, 'Lord,
when did we see You hungry or thirsty or a stranger
or naked or sick or in prison, and did not minister to

You?' Then He will answer them, saying, 'Assuredly, I say to you, inasmuch as you did not do it to one of the least of these, you did not do it to Me.' And these will go away into everlasting punishment, but the righteous into eternal life."

—*Matthew 25:34–46*

Let brotherly love continue. Do not forget to entertain strangers, for by so doing some have unwittingly entertained angels. Remember the prisoners as if chained with them—those who are mistreated—since you yourselves are in the body also.

—*Hebrews 13:1–3*

Is it not to share your bread with the hungry,
And that you bring to your house the poor who
   are cast out;
When you see the naked, that you cover him,
And not hide yourself from your own flesh?
Then your light shall break forth like the morning,
Your healing shall spring forth speedily,
And your righteousness shall go before you;
The glory of the LORD shall be your rear guard.

—*Isaiah 58:7–8*

"And whoever gives one of these little ones only a cup of cold water in the name of a disciple, assuredly, I say to you, he shall by no means lose his reward."

—*Matthew 10:42*

And He said to them, "Go into all the world and preach the gospel to every creature."

—*Mark 16:15*

Beloved, you do faithfully whatever you do for the brethren and for strangers, who have borne witness of your love before the church. If you send them forward on their journey in a manner worthy of God, you will do well.

—*3 John 5–6*

... *with Your Enemies*

"But I say to you who hear: Love your enemies, do good to those who hate you, bless those who curse you, and pray for those who spitefully use you. To him who strikes you on the one cheek, offer the other also. And from him who takes away your cloak, do not withhold your tunic either. Give to everyone who asks of you. And from him who takes away your goods do not ask them back. And just as you want men to do to you, you also do to them likewise."

—*Luke 6:27–31*

Repay no one evil for evil. Have regard for good things in the sight of all men. If it is possible, as much as depends on you, live peaceably with all men. Beloved, do not avenge yourselves, but rather give place to wrath; for it is written, "Vengeance is Mine, I will repay," says the Lord. Therefore

"If your enemy is hungry, feed him;

If he is thirsty, give him a drink;

For in so doing you will heap coals of fire on his head."

Do not be overcome by evil, but overcome evil with good.

—*Romans 12:17–21*

Do not rejoice when your enemy falls,
And do not let your heart be glad when
   he stumbles;
Lest the LORD see it, and it displease Him,
And He turn away His wrath from him.
Do not fret because of evildoers,
Nor be envious of the wicked;
For there will be no prospect for the evil man;
The lamp of the wicked will be put out.

—*Proverbs 24:17–20*

. . . for the LORD your God is He who goes with
you, to fight for you against your enemies, to save
you.

—*Deuteronomy 20:4*

But the Lord is faithful, who will establish you and
guard you from the evil one.

—*2 Thessalonians 3:3*

If your enemy is hungry, give him bread to eat;
And if he is thirsty, give him water to drink;
For so you will heap coals of fire on his head,
And the LORD will reward you.

—*Proverbs 25:21–22*

... *with Your Church*

For where two or three are gathered together in
My name, I am there in the midst of them.

—*Matthew 18:20*

This is the message which we have heard from
Him and declare to you, that God is light and in
Him is no darkness at all. If we say that we have fellowship with Him, and walk in darkness, we lie and
do not practice the truth. But if we walk in the
light as He is in the light, we have fellowship with
one another, and the blood of Jesus Christ His Son
cleanses us from all sin.

—*1 John 1:5–7*

If we live in the Spirit, let us also walk in the Spirit.
Let us not become conceited, provoking one another,
envying one another.

—*Galatians 5:25–26*

And I, brethren, could not speak to you as to spiritual people but as to carnal, as to babes in Christ. I fed
you with milk and not with solid food; for until now

you were not able to receive it, and even now you are still not able; for you are still carnal. For where there are envy, strife, and divisions among you, are you not carnal and behaving like mere men?

—*1 Corinthians 3:1–3*

Therefore take heed to yourselves and to all the flock, among which the Holy Spirit has made you overseers, to shepherd the church of God which He purchased with His own blood. For I know this, that after my departure savage wolves will come in among you, not sparing the flock. Also from among yourselves men will rise up, speaking perverse things, to draw away the disciples after themselves. Therefore watch, and remember that for three years I did not cease to warn everyone night and day with tears. So now, brethren, I commend you to God and to the word of His grace, which is able to build you up and give you an inheritance among all those who are sanctified.

—*Acts 20:28–32*

Nevertheless the solid foundation of God stands, having this seal: "The Lord knows those who are His," and, "Let everyone who names the name of Christ depart from iniquity." But in a great house there are not only vessels of gold and silver, but also of wood and clay, some for honor and some for dishonor. Therefore if anyone cleanses himself from the latter, he will be a vessel for honor, sanctified and useful for the Master, prepared for every good work. Flee also youthful lusts; but pursue righteousness, faith, love, peace with those who call on the Lord out of a pure heart. But avoid foolish and ignorant disputes, knowing that they generate strife. And a servant of the Lord must not quarrel but be gentle to all, able to teach, patient, in humility correcting those who are in opposition, if God perhaps will grant them repentance, so that they may know the truth, and that they may come to their senses and escape the snare of the devil, having been taken captive by him to do his will.

—*2 Timothy 2:19–26*

They zealously court you, but for no good; yes, they want to exclude you, that you may be zealous for them.

—*Galatians 4:17*

No longer do I call you servants, for a servant does not know what his master is doing; but I have called you friends, for all things that I heard from My Father I have made known to you. You did not choose Me, but I chose you and appointed you that you should go and bear fruit, and that your fruit should remain, that whatever you ask the Father in My name He may give you.

—*John 15:15–16*

Deal with Your servant according to Your mercy,
And teach me Your statutes.
I am Your servant;
Give me understanding,
That I may know Your testimonies.

—*Psalm 119:124–125*

He who has My commandments and keeps them,

it is he who loves Me. And he who loves Me will be loved by My Father, and I will love him and manifest Myself to him.

—*John 14:21*

Abide in Me, and I in you. As the branch cannot bear fruit of itself, unless it abides in the vine, neither can you, unless you abide in Me. "I am the vine, you are the branches. He who abides in Me, and I in him, bears much fruit; for without Me you can do nothing. If anyone does not abide in Me, he is cast out as a branch and is withered; and they gather them and throw them into the fire, and they are burned. If you abide in Me, and My words abide in you, you will ask what you desire, and it shall be done for you.

—*John 15:4–7*

In You, O LORD, I put my trust;
Let me never be ashamed;
Deliver me in Your righteousness.
Bow down Your ear to me,
Deliver me speedily;
Be my rock of refuge,
A fortress of defense to save me.
For You are my rock and my fortress;
Therefore, for Your name's sake,

Lead me and guide me.
Pull me out of the net which they have secretly
    laid for me,
For You are my strength.
Into Your hand I commit my spirit;
You have redeemed me, O LORD God of truth.

—Psalm 31:1–5

... with the Poor

He who has pity on the poor lends to the LORD,
And He will pay back what he has given.

—Proverbs 19:17

"If there is among you a poor man of your
brethren, within any of the gates in your land which
the LORD your God is giving you, you shall not
harden your heart nor shut your hand from your
poor brother, but you shall open your hand wide to
him and willingly lend him sufficient for his need,
whatever he needs. Beware lest there be a wicked
thought in your heart, saying, 'The seventh year, the
year of release, is at hand,' and your eye be evil
against your poor brother and you give him nothing, and he cry out to the LORD against you, and it
become sin among you. You shall surely give to him,
and your heart should not be grieved when you give
to him, because for this thing the LORD your God will
bless you in all your works and in all to which you
put your hand. For the poor will never cease from
the land; therefore I command you, saying, 'You shall
open your hand wide to your brother, to your poor
and your needy, in your land.'"

—Deuteronomy 15:7–11

"And whoever gives one of these little ones only a cup of cold water in the name of a disciple, assuredly, I say to you, he shall by no means lose his reward."
—*Matthew 10:42*

But this I say: He who sows sparingly will also reap sparingly, and he who sows bountifully will also reap bountifully. So let each one give as he purposes in his heart, not grudgingly or of necessity; for God loves a cheerful giver. And God is able to make all grace abound toward you, that you, always having all sufficiency in all things, may have an abundance for every good work. As it is written:
"He has dispersed abroad,
He has given to the poor;
His righteousness endures forever."
Now may He who supplies seed to the sower, and bread for food, supply and multiply the seed you have sown and increase the fruits of your righteousness.
—*2 Corinthians 9:6–10*

If a brother or sister is naked and destitute of daily food, and one of you says to them, "Depart in peace, be warmed and filled," but you do not give them the things which are needed for the body, what does it profit?

—*James 2:15–16*

Defend the poor and fatherless;
Do justice to the afflicted and needy.
Deliver the poor and needy;
Free them from the hand of the wicked.

—Psalm 82:3–4

God's Wisdom to
Bless Your Family

. . . that Christ may dwell in your hearts through faith; that you, being rooted and grounded in love, may be able to comprehend with all the saints what is the width and length and depth and height—to know the love of Christ which passes knowledge; that you may be filled with all the fullness of God.

—*Ephesians 3:17–19*

But now, thus says the LORD, who created you,
    O Jacob,
And He who formed you, O Israel:
"Fear not, for I have redeemed you;
I have called you by your name;
You are Mine.
When you pass through the waters, I will be
    with you;
And through the rivers, they shall not
    overflow you.
When you walk through the fire, you shall not
    be burned,
Nor shall the flame scorch you.
For I am the LORD your God,
The Holy One of Israel, your Savior;
I gave Egypt for your ransom,

Ethiopia and Seba in your place.
Since you were precious in My sight,
You have been honored,
And I have loved you;
Therefore I will give men for you,
And people for your life.

—Isaiah 43:1–4

And we know that all things work together for good to those who love God, to those who are the called according to His purpose.

—Romans 8:28

Now hope does not disappoint, because the love of God has been poured out in our hearts by the Holy Spirit who was given to us. . . .

For scarcely for a righteous man will one die; yet perhaps for a good man someone would even dare to die. But God demonstrates His own love toward us, in that while we were still sinners, Christ died for us. Much more then, having now been justified by His blood, we shall be saved from wrath through Him.

—Romans 5:5, 7–9

The LORD your God in your midst,
The Mighty One, will save;

He will rejoice over you with gladness,
He will quiet you with His love,
He will rejoice over you with singing.

—Zephaniah 3:17

Blessed be the LORD,
For He has shown me His marvelous kindness
    in a strong city!
For I said in my haste,
"I am cut off from before Your eyes";
Nevertheless You heard the voice of my
    supplications
When I cried out to You.
Oh, love the LORD, all you His saints!
For the LORD preserves the faithful,
And fully repays the proud person.
Be of good courage,
And He shall strengthen your heart,
All you who hope in the LORD.

—Psalm 31:21–24

But when the kindness and the love of God our
Savior toward man appeared, not by works of righteousness which we have done, but according to His
mercy He saved us, through the washing of regeneration and renewing of the Holy Spirit, whom He
poured out on us abundantly through Jesus Christ

our Savior, that having been justified by His grace we should become heirs according to the hope of eternal life. This is a faithful saying, and these things I want you to affirm constantly, that those who have believed in God should be careful to maintain good works. These things are good and profitable to men.

—*Titus 3:4–8*

With Strength

I can do all things through Christ who strengthens me.

—Philippians 4:13

The LORD is my strength and my shield;
My heart trusted in Him, and I am helped;
Therefore my heart greatly rejoices,
And with my song I will praise Him.
The LORD is their strength,
And He is the saving refuge of His anointed.
Save Your people,
And bless Your inheritance;
Shepherd them also,
And bear them up forever.

—Psalm 28:7–9

Give unto the LORD, O you mighty ones,
Give unto the LORD glory and strength.
Give unto the LORD the glory due to His name;
Worship the LORD in the beauty of holiness.
The voice of the LORD is over the waters;
The God of glory thunders;
The LORD is over many waters.

The voice of the LORD is powerful;
The voice of the LORD is full of majesty. . . .

The voice of the LORD makes the deer give birth,
And strips the forests bare;
And in His temple everyone says, "Glory!"
The LORD sat enthroned at the Flood,
And the LORD sits as King forever.
The LORD will give strength to His people;
The LORD will bless His people with peace.
—Psalm 29:1–4, 9–11

God is our refuge and strength,
A very present help in trouble.
Therefore we will not fear,
Even though the earth be removed,
And though the mountains be carried into
   the midst of the sea;
Though its waters roar and be troubled,
Though the mountains shake with its swelling.
Selah

There is a river whose streams shall make glad
   the city of God,
The holy place of the tabernacle of the Most High.
God is in the midst of her, she shall not be moved;
God shall help her, just at the break of dawn.
—Psalm 46:1–5

Trust in the LORD forever,
For in YAH, the LORD, is everlasting strength.
—*Isaiah 26:4*

Whom have I in heaven but You?
And there is none upon earth that I desire
    besides You.
My flesh and my heart fail;
But God is the strength of my heart and my
    portion forever.
For indeed, those who are far from You
    shall perish;
You have destroyed all those who desert You
    for harlotry.
But it is good for me to draw near to God;
I have put my trust in the Lord GOD,
That I may declare all Your works.
—*Psalm 73:25–28*

    And He said to me, "My grace is sufficient for you,
for My strength is made perfect in weakness." Therefore most gladly I will rather boast in my infirmities,
that the power of Christ may rest upon me. Therefore I take pleasure in infirmities, in reproaches, in
needs, in persecutions, in distresses, for Christ's sake.
For when I am weak, then I am strong.
—*2 Corinthians 12:9–10*

Fear not, for I am with you;
Be not dismayed, for I am your God.
I will strengthen you,
Yes, I will help you,
I will uphold you with My righteous
right hand.

—Isaiah 41:10

With Joy

Though the fig tree may not blossom,
Nor fruit be on the vines;
Though the labor of the olive may fail,
And the fields yield no food;
Though the flock may be cut off from the fold,
And there be no herd in the stalls—
Yet I will rejoice in the LORD,
I will joy in the God of my salvation.
The LORD God is my strength;
He will make my feet like deer's feet,
And He will make me walk on my high hills.
                              —*Habakkuk 3:17–19a*

But let all those rejoice who put their trust in You;
Let them ever shout for joy, because You defend them;
Let those also who love Your name
Be joyful in You.
For You, O LORD, will bless the righteous;
With favor You will surround him as with a shield.
                              —*Psalm 5:11–12*

If you keep My commandments, you will abide in
My love, just as I have kept My Father's command-

ments and abide in His love. "These things I have spoken to you, that My joy may remain in you, and that your joy may be full.

—*John 15:10–11*

Then he said to them, "Go your way, eat the fat, drink the sweet, and send portions to those for whom nothing is prepared; for this day is holy to our Lord. Do not sorrow, for the joy of the Lord is your strength."So the Levites quieted all the people, saying, "Be still, for the day is holy; do not be grieved." And all the people went their way to eat and drink, to send portions and rejoice greatly, because they understood the words that were declared to them.

—*Nehemiah 8:10–12*

Then the angel said to them, "Do not be afraid, for behold, I bring you good tidings of great joy which will be to all people. For there is born to you this day in the city of David a Savior, who is Christ the Lord. And this will be the sign to you: You will find a Babe wrapped in swaddling cloths, lying in a manger." And suddenly there was with the angel a multitude of the heavenly host praising God and saying: "Glory to God in the highest, and on earth peace, goodwill toward men!"

—*Luke 2:10–14*

For the LORD will comfort Zion,
He will comfort all her waste places;
He will make her wilderness like Eden,
And her desert like the garden of the Lord;
Joy and gladness will be found in it,
Thanksgiving and the voice of melody. . . .
So the ransomed of the Lord shall return,
And come to Zion with singing,
With everlasting joy on their heads.
They shall obtain joy and gladness;
Sorrow and sighing shall flee away.

—*Isaiah 51:3, 11*

Now Jesus knew that they desired to ask Him, and He said to them, "Are you inquiring among your-selves about what I said, 'A little while, and you will not see Me; and again a little while, and you will see Me'? Most assuredly, I say to you that you will weep and lament, but the world will rejoice; and you will be sorrowful, but your sorrow will be turned into joy. A woman, when she is in labor, has sorrow because her hour has come; but as soon as she has given birth to the child, she no longer remembers the anguish, for joy that a human being has been born into the world. Therefore you now have sorrow; but I will see you again and your heart will rejoice, and your joy no one will take from you."

—*John 16:19–22*

With Fruitfulness

"I am the true vine, and My Father is the vine-dresser. Every branch in Me that does not bear fruit He takes away; and every branch that bears fruit He prunes, that it may bear more fruit. You are already clean because of the word which I have spoken to you. Abide in Me, and I in you. As the branch cannot bear fruit of itself, unless it abides in the vine, neither can you, unless you abide in Me. I am the vine, you are the branches. He who abides in Me, and I in him, bears much fruit; for without Me you can do nothing. If anyone does not abide in Me, he is cast out as a branch and is withered; and they gather them and throw them into the fire, and they are burned. If you abide in Me, and My words abide in you, you will ask what you desire, and it shall be done for you. By this My Father is glorified, that you bear much fruit; so you will be My disciples. As the Father loved Me, I also have loved you; abide in My love."

—*John 15:1–9*

But the fruit of the Spirit is love, joy, peace, long-suffering, kindness, goodness, faithfulness, gentleness, self-control. Against such there is no law. And those who are Christ's have crucified the flesh with its passions and desires. If we live in the Spirit, let us also walk in the Spirit. Let us not become conceited, provoking one another, envying one another.

—Galatians 5:22–26

For this reason we also, since the day we heard it, do not cease to pray for you, and to ask that you may be filled with the knowledge of His will in all wisdom and spiritual understanding; that you may walk worthy of the Lord, fully pleasing Him, being fruitful in every good work and increasing in the knowledge of God.

—Colossians 1:9–10

My fruit is better than gold, yes, than fine gold,
And my revenue than choice silver.
I traverse the way of righteousness,
In the midst of the paths of justice,
That I may cause those who love me to inherit wealth,
That I may fill their treasuries.

—Proverbs 8:19–21

What is man that You are mindful of him,
And the son of man that You visit him?
For You have made him a little lower than the angels,
And You have crowned him with glory and honor.

You have made him to have dominion over the
works of Your hands;
You have put all things under his feet,
All sheep and oxen—
Even the beasts of the field,
The birds of the air,
And the fish of the sea
That pass through the paths of the seas.
O LORD, our Lord,
How excellent is Your name in all the earth!
—*Psalm 8:4–9*

Your wife shall be like a fruitful vine
In the very heart of your house,
Your children like olive plants
All around your table.

—*Psalm 128:3*

Ask of Me, and I will give You
The nations for Your inheritance,
And the ends of the earth for Your possession.
—*Psalm 2:8*

For I will look on you favorably and make you fruitful, multiply you and confirm My covenant with you.
—*Leviticus 26:9*

And He said, "My Presence will go with you, and I will give you rest."

—*Exodus 33:14*

. . . whom God raised up, having loosed the pains of death, because it was not possible that He should be held by it. For David says concerning Him:
"I foresaw the LORD always before my face,
For He is at my right hand, that I may not be shaken.
Therefore my heart rejoiced, and my tongue
    was glad;
Moreover my flesh also will rest in hope.
For You will not leave my soul in Hades,
Nor will You allow Your Holy One to see
    corruption."

—*Acts 2:24–27*

"Come to Me, all you who labor and are heavy laden, and I will give you rest. Take My yoke upon you and learn from Me, for I am gentle and lowly in heart, and you will find rest for your souls. For My yoke is easy and My burden is light."

—*Matthew 11:28–30*

The LORD preserves the simple;
I was brought low, and He saved me.
Return to your rest, O my soul,
For the LORD has dealt bountifully with you.

—Psalm 116:6–7

. . . for as yet you have not come to the rest and
the inheritance which the LORD your God is giving
you. But when you cross over the Jordan and dwell in
the land which the LORD your God is giving you to
inherit, and He gives you rest from all your enemies
round about, so that you dwell in safety.

—Deuteronomy 12:9–10

Rest in the LORD, and wait patiently for Him;
Do not fret because of him who prospers in
    his way,
Because of the man who brings wicked schemes
    to pass.
Cease from anger, and forsake wrath;
Do not fret—it only causes harm.

—Psalm 37:7–8

For he who has entered His rest has himself also
ceased from his works as God did from His.
Let us therefore be diligent to enter that rest, lest

anyone fall according to the same example of disobedience. For the word of God is living and powerful, and sharper than any two-edged sword, piercing even to the division of soul and spirit, and of joints and marrow, and is a discerner of the thoughts and intents of the heart.

—*Hebrews 4:10–12*

GOD'S WISDOM TO BLESS YOUR FAMILY
With His Spirit

Beloved, if God so loved us, we also ought to love one another.

No one has seen God at any time. If we love one another, God abides in us, and His love has been perfected in us. By this we know that we abide in Him, and He in us, because He has given us of His Spirit.

—1 John 4:11–13

But you are not in the flesh but in the Spirit, if indeed the Spirit of God dwells in you. Now if anyone does not have the Spirit of Christ, he is not His. And if Christ is in you, the body is dead because of sin, but the Spirit is life because of righteousness. But if the Spirit of Him who raised Jesus from the dead dwells in you, He who raised Christ from the dead will also give life to your mortal bodies through His Spirit who dwells in you.

Therefore, brethren, we are debtors—not to the flesh, to live according to the flesh. For if you live according to the flesh you will die; but if by the Spirit you put to death the deeds of the body, you will live. For as many as are led by the Spirit of God, these are sons of God. For you did not receive the spirit of bondage again to fear, but you received the Spirit of adoption by whom we cry out, "Abba, Father." The Spirit Himself bears witness with our spirit that we are children of God,

—*Romans 8:9–16*

For our gospel did not come to you in word only, but also in power, and in the Holy Spirit and in much assurance, as you know what kind of men we were among you for your sake.

—*1 Thessalonians 1:5*

Do you not know that you are the temple of God and that the Spirit of God dwells in you?

—*1 Corinthians 3:16*

Behold, the eye of the LORD is on those who fear Him,
On those who hope in His mercy,
To deliver their soul from death,
And to keep them alive in famine.
Our soul waits for the LORD;
He is our help and our shield.
For our heart shall rejoice in Him,
Because we have trusted in His holy name.
Let Your mercy, O LORD, be upon us,
Just as we hope in You.

—*Psalm 33:18–22*

Now he who keeps His commandments abides in Him, and He in him. And by this we know that He abides in us, by the Spirit whom He has given us.

—*1 John 3:24*

. . . who also has sealed us and given us the Spirit in our hearts as a guarantee.

—*2 Corinthians 1:22*

But God has revealed them to us through His Spirit. For the Spirit searches all things, yes, the deep things of God. For what man knows the things of a man except the spirit of the man which is in him? Even so no one knows the things of God except the Spirit of God. Now we have received, not the spirit of the world, but the Spirit who is from God, that we might know the things that have been freely given to us by God. These things we also speak, not in words which man's wisdom teaches but which the Holy Spirit teaches, comparing spiritual things with spiritual. But the natural man does not receive the things of the Spirit of God, for they are foolishness to him; nor can he know them, because they are spiritually discerned. But he who is spiritual judges all things, yet he himself is rightly judged by no one. For "who has known the mind of the Lord that he may instruct Him?" But we have the mind of Christ.

—*1 Corinthians 2:10–16*

The spirit of a man is the lamp of the LORD,
Searching all the inner depths of his heart.
—*Proverbs 20:27*

Not that we are sufficient of ourselves to think of anything as being from ourselves, but our sufficiency is from God, who also made us sufficient as ministers of the new covenant, not of the letter but of the Spirit; for the letter kills, but the Spirit gives life.
—*2 Corinthians 3:5–6*

With Hope

Now may the God of hope fill you with all joy and peace in believing, that you may abound in hope by the power of the Holy Spirit.

—Romans 15:13

Beloved, now we are children of God; and it has not yet been revealed what we shall be, but we know that when He is revealed, we shall be like Him, for we shall see Him as He is. And everyone who has this hope in Him purifies himself, just as He is pure.

—1 John 3:2–3

For I consider that the sufferings of this present time are not worthy to be compared with the glory which shall be revealed in us. For the earnest expectation of the creation eagerly waits for the revealing of the sons of God. . . .

For we were saved in this hope, but hope that is seen is not hope; for why does one still hope for what he sees? But if we hope for what we do not see, we eagerly wait for it with perseverance.

—Romans 8:18–19, 24–25

"These things I have spoken to you, that in Me you may have peace. In the world you will have tribulation; but be of good cheer, I have overcome the world."

—*John 16:33*

Behold, the eye of the LORD is on those who
  fear Him,
On those who hope in His mercy,
To deliver their soul from death,
And to keep them alive in famine.
Our soul waits for the LORD;
He is our help and our shield.
For our heart shall rejoice in Him,
Because we have trusted in His holy name.
Let Your mercy, O LORD, be upon us,
Just as we hope in You.

—*Psalm 33:18–22*

Through the LORD's mercies we are not consumed,
Because His compassions fail not.
They are new every morning;
Great is Your faithfulness.
"The LORD is my portion," says my soul,
"Therefore I hope in Him!"

—*Lamentations 3:22–24*

The mystery which has been hidden from ages and from generations, ... now has been revealed to His saints. To them God willed to make known what are the riches of the glory of this mystery among the Gentiles: which is Christ in you, the hope of glory.

—*Colossians 1:26–27*

... with all lowliness and gentleness, with long-suffering, bearing with one another in love, endeavoring to keep the unity of the Spirit in the bond of peace. There is one body and one Spirit, just as you were called in one hope of your calling; one Lord, one faith, one baptism; one God and Father of all, who is above all, and through all, and in you all.

—*Ephesians 4:2–6*

With Guidance

Thus says the LORD, your Redeemer,
The Holy One of Israel:
"I am the LORD your God,
Who teaches you to profit,
Who leads you by the way you should go.

—Isaiah 48:17

Commit your works to the LORD,
And your thoughts will be established.

—Proverbs 16:3

The LORD will guide you continually,
And satisfy your soul in drought,
And strengthen your bones;
You shall be like a watered garden,
And like a spring of water, whose waters do not fail.

—Isaiah 58:11

"I, the LORD, have called You in righteousness,
And will hold Your hand;
I will keep You and give You as a covenant to the people,
As a light to the Gentiles.

—Isaiah 42:6

Trust in the LORD with all your heart,
And lean not on your own understanding;
In all your ways acknowledge Him,
And He shall direct your paths.

—Proverbs 3:5–6

I will instruct you and teach you in the way
    you should go;
I will guide you with My eye.

—Psalm 32:8

I will put My Spirit within you and cause you to
walk in My statutes, and you will keep My judgments
and do them.

—Ezekiel 36:27

"However, when He, the Spirit of truth, has come,
He will guide you into all truth; for He will not speak
on His own authority, but whatever He hears He will
speak; and He will tell you things to come."

—John 16:13

For this is God,
Our God forever and ever;
He will be our guide
Even to death.

—Psalm 48:14

God's Wisdom That Will Change Your Life

With Repentance

From that time Jesus began to preach and to say, "Repent, for the kingdom of heaven is at hand."
—*Matthew 4:17*

"Now, therefore," says the LORD,
"Turn to Me with all your heart,
With fasting, with weeping, and with mourning."
So rend your heart, and not your garments;
Return to the LORD your God,
For He is gracious and merciful,
Slow to anger, and of great kindness;
And He relents from doing harm.

—*Joel 2:12–13*

And do you think this, O man, you who judge those practicing such things, and doing the same, that you will escape the judgment of God? Or do you despise the riches of His goodness, forbearance, and longsuffering, not knowing that the goodness of God leads you to repentance?

—*Romans 2:3–4*

"Take heed to yourselves. If your brother sins against you, rebuke him; and if he repents, forgive him. And if he sins against you seven times in a day, and seven times in a day returns to you, saying, 'I repent,' you shall forgive him."

—*Luke 17:3–4*

For if in anything I have boasted to him about you, I am not ashamed. But as we spoke all things to you in truth, even so our boasting to Titus was found true.

—*2 Corinthians 7:14*

Come, and let us return to the LORD;
For He has torn, but He will heal us;
He has stricken, but He will bind us up.

—*Hosea 6:1*

Then Peter said to them, "Repent, and let every one of you be baptized in the name of Jesus Christ for the remission of sins; and you shall receive the gift of the Holy Spirit."

—*Acts 2:38*

With Forgiveness

If we say that we have fellowship with Him, and walk in darkness, we lie and do not practice the truth. But if we walk in the light as He is in the light, we have fellowship with one another, and the blood of Jesus Christ His Son cleanses us from all sin. If we say that we have no sin, we deceive ourselves, and the truth is not in us. If we confess our sins, He is faithful and just to forgive us our sins and to cleanse us from all unrighteousness. If we say that we have not sinned, we make Him a liar, and His word is not in us.

—*1 John 1:6–10*

But if anyone has caused grief, he has not grieved me, but all of you to some extent—not to be too severe. This punishment which was inflicted by the majority is sufficient for such a man, so that, on the contrary, you ought rather to forgive and comfort him, lest perhaps such a one be swallowed up with too much sorrow. Therefore I urge you to reaffirm your love to him. For to this end I also wrote, that I might put you to the test, whether you are obedient in all things. Now whom you forgive anything, I also forgive. For if indeed I have forgiven anything, I have forgiven that one for your sakes in the presence of Christ, lest Satan should take advantage of us; for we are not ignorant of his devices.

—*2 Corinthians 2:5–11*

"And whenever you stand praying, if you have anything against anyone, forgive him, that your Father in heaven may also forgive you your trespasses. But if you do not forgive, neither will your Father in heaven forgive your trespasses."

—*Mark 11:25–26*

"I, even I, am He who blots out your transgressions
   for My own sake;
And I will not remember your sins."

—*Isaiah 43:25*

Let all bitterness, wrath, anger, clamor, and evil speaking be put away from you, with all malice. And be kind to one another, tenderhearted, forgiving one another, even as God in Christ forgave you.

—*Ephesians 4:31–32*

If You, Lord, should mark iniquities,
O Lord, who could stand?

But there is forgiveness with You,
That You may be feared.
I wait for the LORD, my soul waits.

—*Psalm 130:3–5a*

My brethren, count it all joy when you fall into various trials, knowing that the testing of your faith produces patience. But let patience have its perfect work, that you may be perfect and complete, lacking nothing.

—*James 1:2–4*

Therefore we also, since we are surrounded by so great a cloud of witnesses, let us lay aside every weight, and the sin which so easily ensnares us, and let us run with endurance the race that is set before us.

—*Hebrews 12:1*

And not only that, but we also glory in tribulations, knowing that tribulation produces perseverance; and perseverance, character; and character, hope.

—*Romans 5:3–4*

For even Christ did not please Himself; but as it is written, "The reproaches of those who reproached You fell on Me." For whatever things were written before were written for our learning, that we through the patience and comfort of the Scriptures might have hope. Now may the God of patience and comfort grant you to be like-minded toward one another, according to Christ Jesus, that you may with one mind and one mouth glorify the God and Father of our Lord Jesus Christ.

—*Romans 15:3–6*

For the love of money is a root of all kinds of evil, for which some have strayed from the faith in their greediness, and pierced themselves through with many sorrows.

But you, O man of God, flee these things and pursue righteousness, godliness, faith, love, patience, gentleness.

—*1 Timothy 6:10–11*

Now faith is the substance of things hoped for, the evidence of things not seen. For by it the elders obtained a good testimony. By faith we understand that the worlds were framed by the word of God, so that the things which are seen were not made of things which are visible.

By faith Abel offered to God a more excellent sacrifice than Cain, through which he obtained witness that he was righteous, God testifying of his gifts; and through it he being dead still speaks. By faith Enoch was taken away so that he did not see death, "and was not found, because God had taken him"; for before he was taken he had this testimony, that he pleased God. But without faith it is impossible to please Him, for he who comes to God must believe that He is, and that He is a rewarder of those who diligently seek Him. By faith Noah, being divinely warned of things not yet seen, moved with godly fear, prepared an ark for the saving of his household, by which he condemned the world and became heir of the righteousness which is according to faith.

By faith Abraham obeyed when he was called to go out to the place which he would receive as an inheritance. And he went out, not knowing where he was going. By faith he dwelt in the land of promise as in a foreign country, dwelling in tents with Isaac and Jacob, the heirs with him of the same promise; for he waited for the city which has foundations, whose builder and maker is God. By faith Sarah herself also received strength to conceive seed, and she bore a child when she was past the age, because she judged Him faithful who had promised. Therefore from one man, and him as good as dead, were born as many as the stars of the sky in multitude—innumerable as the sand which is by the seashore.

These all died in faith, not having received the promises, but having seen them afar off were assured of them, embraced them and confessed that they were strangers and pilgrims on the earth.

—*Hebrews 11:1–13*

But the Scripture has confined all under sin, that the promise by faith in Jesus Christ might be given to those who believe. But before faith came, we were kept under guard by the law, kept for the faith which would afterward be revealed. Therefore the law was our tutor to bring us to Christ, that we might be justified by faith. But after faith has come, we are no longer under a tutor.

For you are all sons of God through faith in Christ Jesus.

—*Galatians 3:22–26*

For I am not ashamed of the gospel of Christ, for it is the power of God to salvation for everyone who believes, for the Jew first and also for the Greek. For in it the righteousness of God is revealed from faith to faith; as it is written, "The just shall live by faith."

—*Romans 1:16–17*

Watch, stand fast in the faith, be brave, be strong. Let all that you do be done with love.

—*1 Corinthians 16:13–14*

. . . and the father of circumcision to those who not only are of the circumcision, but who also walk in the steps of the faith which our father Abraham had while still uncircumcised.

For the promise that he would be the heir of the world was not to Abraham or to his seed through the law, but through the righteousness of faith. For if those who are of the law are heirs, faith is made void and the promise made of no effect, because the law brings about wrath; for where there is no law there is no transgression. Therefore it is of faith that it might be according to grace, so that the promise might be sure to all the seed, not only to those who are of the law, but also to those who are of the faith of Abraham, who is the father of us all (as it is written, "I have made you a father of many nations") in the presence of Him whom he believed—God, who gives life to the dead and calls those things which do not exist as though they did; who, contrary to hope, in hope believed, so that he became the father of many nations, according to what was spoken, "So shall your descendants be." And not being weak in faith, he did not consider his own body, already dead (since he was about a hundred years old), and the deadness of Sarah's womb. He did not waver at the promise of God through unbelief, but was strengthened in faith, giving glory to God, and being fully convinced that what He had promised He was also able to perform.

—*Romans 4:12–21*

So Jesus said to them, "Because of your unbelief; for assuredly, I say to you, if you have faith as a mustard seed, you will say to this mountain, 'Move from here to there,' and it will move; and nothing will be impossible for you."

—*Matthew 17:20*

For we do not wrestle against flesh and blood, but against principalities, against powers, against the rulers of the darkness of this age, against spiritual hosts of wickedness in the heavenly places. Therefore take up the whole armor of God, that you may be able to withstand in the evil day, and having done all, to stand. Stand therefore, having girded your waist with truth, having put on the breastplate of righteousness, and having shod your feet with the preparation of the gospel of peace; above all, taking the shield of faith with which you will be able to quench all the fiery darts of the wicked one.

—*Ephesians 6:12–16*

With Good Works

The righteous shall flourish like a palm tree,
He shall grow like a cedar in Lebanon.
Those who are planted in the house of the LORD
Shall flourish in the courts of our God.
They shall still bear fruit in old age;
They shall be fresh and flourishing.

—*Psalm 92:12–14*

Blessed are the undefiled in the way,
Who walk in the law of the Lord!
Blessed are those who keep His testimonies,
Who seek Him with the whole heart!
They also do no iniquity;
They walk in His ways.

—*Psalm 119:1–3*

But above all these things put on love, which is
the bond of perfection. And let the peace of God rule
in your hearts, to which also you were called in one
body; and be thankful. Let the word of Christ dwell
in you richly in all wisdom, teaching and admonish-
ing one another in psalms and hymns and spiritual

songs, singing with grace in your hearts to the Lord. And whatever you do in word or deed, do all in the name of the Lord Jesus, giving thanks to God the Father through Him.

—Colossians 3:14–17

And let us not grow weary while doing good, for in due season we shall reap if we do not lose heart. Therefore, as we have opportunity, let us do good to all, especially to those who are of the household of faith.

—Galatians 6:9–10

Who is the man who desires life,
And loves many days, that he may see good?
Keep your tongue from evil,
And your lips from speaking deceit.
Depart from evil and do good;
Seek peace and pursue it.
The eyes of the LORD are on the righteous,
And His ears are open to their cry.

—Psalm 34:12–15

"Most assuredly, I say to you, he who believes in Me, the works that I do he will do also; and greater works than these he will do, because I go to My Father."

—John 14:12

With Obedience

"I beseech you therefore, brethren, by the mercies of God, that you present your bodies a living sacrifice, holy, acceptable to God, which is your reasonable service. And do not be conformed to this world, but be transformed by the renewing of your mind, that you may prove what is that good and acceptable and perfect will of God.

—Romans 12:1–2

But this is what I commanded them, saying, "Obey My voice, and I will be your God, and you shall be My people. And walk in all the ways that I have commanded you, that it may be well with you."

—Jeremiah 7:23

"He who has My commandments and keeps them, it is he who loves Me. And he who loves Me will be loved by My Father, and I will love him and manifest Myself to him."

—John 14:21

"Now therefore, if you will indeed obey My voice and keep My covenant, then you shall be a special treasure to Me above all people; for all the earth is Mine."

—Exodus 19:5

Teach me, O LORD, the way of Your statutes,
And I shall keep it to the end.
Give me understanding, and I shall keep Your law;
Indeed, I shall observe it with my whole heart.

—Psalm 119:33–34

"Then I will give them one heart, and I will put a new spirit within them, and take the stony heart out of their flesh, and give them a heart of flesh, that they may walk in My statutes and keep My judgments and do them; and they shall be My people, and I will be their God."

—Ezekiel 11:19–20

Therefore gird up the loins of your mind, be sober, and rest your hope fully upon the grace that is to be brought to you at the revelation of Jesus Christ; as obedient children, not conforming yourselves to the former lusts, as in your ignorance; but as He who called you is holy, you also be holy in all your conduct, because it is written, "Be holy, for I am holy."

—1 Peter 1:13–16

And this I pray, that your love may abound still more and more in knowledge and all discernment, that you may approve the things that are excellent, that you may be sincere and without offense till the day of Christ, being filled with the fruits of righteousness which are by Jesus Christ, to the glory and praise of God.

—Philippians 1:9–11

Your hands have made me and fashioned me; Give me understanding, that I may learn Your commandments.

—Psalm 119:73

Whoever loves instruction loves knowledge, But he who hates correction is stupid.

—Proverbs 12:1

A scoffer seeks wisdom and does not find it, But knowledge is easy to him who understands. Go from the presence of a foolish man,

When you do not perceive in him the lips
    of knowledge.
The wisdom of the prudent is to understand
    his way,
But the folly of fools is deceit.

                    —Proverbs 14:6–8

Wisdom is good with an inheritance,
And profitable to those who see the sun.
For wisdom is a defense as money is a defense,
But the excellence of knowledge is that wisdom
gives life to those who have it.

                    —Ecclesiastes 7:11–12

With Kindness

Let all bitterness, wrath, anger, clamor, and evil speaking be put away from you, with all malice. And be kind to one another, tenderhearted, forgiving one another, even as God in Christ forgave you.

—Ephesians 4:31–32

O God, You are my God;
Early will I seek You;
My soul thirsts for You;
My flesh longs for You
In a dry and thirsty land
Where there is no water.
So I have looked for You in the sanctuary,
To see Your power and Your glory.
Because Your lovingkindness is better than life,
My lips shall praise You.
Thus I will bless You while I live;
I will lift up my hands in Your name.

—Psalm 63:1–4

But the end of all things is at hand; therefore be serious and watchful in your prayers. And above all things have fervent love for one another, for "love will cover a multitude of sins."

—*1 Peter 4:7–8*

Finally, all of you be of one mind, having compassion for one another; love as brothers, be tenderhearted, be courteous; not returning evil for evil or reviling for reviling, but on the contrary blessing, knowing that you were called to this, that you may inherit a blessing.

—*1 Peter 3:8–9*

Now we exhort you, brethren, warn those who are unruly, comfort the fainthearted, uphold the weak, be patient with all. See that no one renders evil for evil to anyone, but always pursue what is good both for yourselves and for all. Rejoice always, pray without ceasing, in everything give thanks; for this is the will of God in Christ Jesus for you.

—*1 Thessalonians 5:14–18*

Praise the LORD, all you Gentiles! Laud Him, all
    you peoples!
For His merciful kindness is great toward us,
And the truth of the LORD endures forever.
Praise the LORD!

—*Psalm 117:1–2*

God's Wisdom
Will Protect You

God's Wisdom Will Protect You
From Evil

The LORD is my shepherd; I shall not want.
He makes me to lie down in green pastures;
He leads me beside the still waters.
He restores my soul;
He leads me in the paths of righteousness
For His name's sake.
Yea, though I walk through the valley of the
shadow of death,
I will fear no evil;
For You are with me;
Your rod and Your staff, they comfort me.
—*Psalm 23:1–4*

No temptation has overtaken you except such as is common to man; but God is faithful, who will not allow you to be tempted beyond what you are able, but with the temptation will also make the way of escape, that you may be able to bear it.
—*1 Corinthians 10:13*

Therefore submit to God. Resist the devil and he will flee from you.
—*James 4:7*

The Lord knows how to deliver the godly out of temptations and to reserve the unjust under punishment for the day of judgment.

—*2 Peter 2:9*

For You are not a God who takes pleasure in wickedness,
Nor shall evil dwell with You.
The boastful shall not stand in Your sight;
You hate all workers of iniquity.
You shall destroy those who speak falsehood;
The LORD abhors the bloodthirsty and deceitful man.
But as for me, I will come into Your house in the
    multitude of Your mercy;
In fear of You I will worship toward Your holy temple.

—*Psalm 5:4–7*

The blessing of the LORD makes one rich,
And He adds no sorrow with it.
To do evil is like sport to a fool,
But a man of understanding has wisdom.

—*Proverbs 10:22–23*

No evil shall befall you,
Nor shall any plague come near your dwelling;
For He shall give His angels charge over you,
To keep you in all your ways.

—*Psalm 91:10–11*

GOD'S WISDOM WILL PROTECT YOU
From Despair

The LORD is my rock and my fortress and
   my deliverer;
My God, my strength, in whom I will trust;
My shield and the horn of my salvation,
   my stronghold.
I will call upon the LORD, who is worthy to
   be praised;
So shall I be saved from my enemies.
The pangs of death surrounded me,
And the floods of ungodliness made me afraid.
The sorrows of Sheol surrounded me;
The snares of death confronted me.
In my distress I called upon the Lord,
And cried out to my God;
He heard my voice from His temple,
And my cry came before Him, even to His ears.
                                    —*Psalm 18:2–6*

Let the redeemed of the LORD say so,
Whom He has redeemed from the hand of
   the enemy,
And gathered out of the lands,
From the east and from the west,
From the north and from the south.

They wandered in the wilderness in a desolate way;
They found no city to dwell in.
Hungry and thirsty,
Their soul fainted in them.
Then they cried out to the LORD in their trouble,
And He delivered them out of their distresses.
And He led them forth by the right way,
That they might go to a city for a dwelling place.
Oh, that men would give thanks to the LORD for
    His goodness,
And for His wonderful works to the children
    of men!
For He satisfies the longing soul,
And fills the hungry soul with goodness.

—Psalm 107:2–9

Then they cried out to the LORD in their trouble,
And He saved them out of their distresses.
He brought them out of darkness and the shadow
    of death,
And broke their chains in pieces.
Oh, that men would give thanks to the LORD for
    His goodness,
And for His wonderful works to the children
    of men!

—Psalm 107:13–15

Do not withhold Your tender mercies from me,
    O Lord;
Let Your lovingkindness and Your truth continually
    preserve me.
For innumerable evils have surrounded me;
My iniquities have overtaken me, so that I am not
    able to look up;
They are more than the hairs of my head;
Therefore my heart fails me.
Be pleased, O Lord, to deliver me;
O Lord, make haste to help me!
Let them be ashamed and brought to mutual
    confusion
Who seek to destroy my life;
Let them be driven backward and brought
    to dishonor
Who wish me evil.
Let them be confounded because of their shame,
Who say to me, "Aha, aha!"
Let all those who seek You rejoice and be glad
    in You;
Let such as love Your salvation say continually,
"The Lord be magnified!"
But I am poor and needy;
Yet the Lord thinks upon me.
You are my help and my deliverer;
Do not delay, O my God.

—*Psalm 40:11–17*

Then you shall call, and the LORD will answer;
You shall cry, and He will say, "Here I am."
If you take away the yoke from your midst,
The pointing of the finger, and speaking
    wickedness,
If you extend your soul to the hungry
And satisfy the afflicted soul,
Then your light shall dawn in the darkness,
And your darkness shall be as the noonday.
The LORD will guide you continually,
And satisfy your soul in drought,
And strengthen your bones;
You shall be like a watered garden,
And like a spring of water, whose waters do
    not fail.
Those from among you
Shall build the old waste places;
You shall raise up the foundations of many
    generations;
And you shall be called the Repairer of the Breach,
The Restorer of Streets to Dwell In.

—Isaiah 58:9–12

GOD'S WISDOM WILL PROTECT YOU
From Harm

Give ear, O LORD, to my prayer;
And attend to the voice of my supplications.
In the day of my trouble I will call upon You,
For You will answer me.

—Psalm 86:6–7

Unless the LORD builds the house,
They labor in vain who build it;
Unless the LORD guards the city,
The watchman stays awake in vain.

—Psalm 127:1

"Therefore do not worry about tomorrow, for tomorrow will worry about its own things. Sufficient
for the day is its own trouble."

—Matthew 6:34

Then the earth shook and trembled;
The foundations of the hills also quaked and
    were shaken,
Because He was angry.
Smoke went up from His nostrils,

And devouring fire from His mouth;
Coals were kindled by it.
He bowed the heavens also, and came down
With darkness under His feet.

—*Psalm 18:7–9*

Therefore submit to God. Resist the devil and he will flee from you. Draw near to God and He will draw near to you. Cleanse your hands, you sinners; and purify your hearts, you double-minded.

Humble yourselves in the sight of the Lord, and He will lift you up.

—*James 4:7–8, 10*

What shall we say then? Shall we continue in sin that grace may abound? Certainly not! How shall we who died to sin live any longer in it? Or do you not know that as many of us as were baptized into Christ Jesus were baptized into His death? Therefore we were buried with Him through baptism into death, that just as Christ was raised from the dead by the glory of the Father, even so we also should walk in newness of life. For if we have been united together in the likeness of His death, certainly we also shall be in the likeness of His resurrection, knowing this, that our old man was crucified with Him, that the body of sin might be done away with, that we should no longer be slaves of sin. For he who has died has been freed from sin. Now if we died with Christ, we believe that we shall also live with Him. . . .

Therefore do not let sin reign in your mortal body, that you should obey it in its lusts. And do not present your members as instruments of unrighteousness to sin, but present yourselves to God as being alive from the dead, and your members as instruments of righteousness to God. For sin shall not have dominion over you, for you are not under law but under grace.

—Romans 6:1–8, 12–14

From Sin

There is therefore now no condemnation to those who are in Christ Jesus, who do not walk according to the flesh, but according to the Spirit. For the law of the Spirit of life in Christ Jesus has made me free from the law of sin and death.

—*Romans 8:1–2*

. . . knowing that Christ, having been raised from the dead, dies no more. Death no longer has dominion over Him. For the death that He died, He died to sin once for all; but the life that He lives, He lives to God. Likewise you also, reckon yourselves to be dead indeed to sin, but alive to God in Christ Jesus our Lord. Therefore do not let sin reign in your mortal body, that you should obey it in its lusts. And do not present your members as instruments of unrighteousness to sin, but present yourselves to God as being alive from the dead, and your members as instruments of righteousness to God. For sin shall not have dominion over you, for you are not under law but under grace.

What then? Shall we sin because we are not under law but under grace? Certainly not! Do you not know that to whom you present yourselves slaves to obey, you are that one's slaves whom you obey, whether of sin leading to death, or of obedience leading to righteousness? But God be thanked that though you were slaves of sin, yet you obeyed from the heart that form of doctrine to which you were delivered. And having been set free from sin, you became slaves of righteousness.

—*Romans 6:9–18*

Therefore let him who thinks he stands take heed lest he fall. No temptation has overtaken you except such as is common to man; but God is faithful, who will not allow you to be tempted beyond what you are able, but with the temptation will also make the way of escape, that you may be able to bear it.

—*1 Corinthians 10:12–13*

What shall we say then? Shall we continue in sin that grace may abound? Certainly not! How shall we who died to sin live any longer in it? Or do you not know that as many of us as were baptized into Christ Jesus were baptized into His death? Therefore we were buried with Him through baptism into death, that just as Christ was raised from the dead by the glory of the Father, even so we also should walk in newness of life. For if we have been united together in the likeness of His death, certainly we also shall be in the likeness of His resurrection, knowing this, that our old man was crucified with Him, that the body of sin might be done away with, that we should no longer be slaves of sin. For he who has died has been freed from sin. Now if we died with Christ, we believe that we shall also live with Him.

—*Romans 6:1–8*

My little children, these things I write to you, so that you may not sin. And if anyone sins, we have an Advocate with the Father, Jesus Christ the righteous. And He Himself is the propitiation for our sins, and not for ours only but also for the whole world.

But whoever keeps His word, truly the love of God is perfected in him. By this we know that we are in Him.

—*1 John 2:1–2, 5*

We implore you on Christ's behalf, be reconciled to God. For He made Him who knew no sin to be sin for us, that we might become the righteousness of God in Him.

—*2 Corinthians 5:20b–21*

GOD'S WISDOM WILL PROTECT YOU
From Enemies

Arise, O LORD, in Your anger;
Lift Yourself up because of the rage of my enemies;
Rise up for me to the judgment You have
    commanded!
So the congregation of the peoples shall
    surround You;
For their sakes, therefore, return on high.
The LORD shall judge the peoples;
Judge me, O LORD, according to my righteousness,
And according to my integrity within me.
                                        —*Psalm 7:6–8*

I will love You, O LORD, my strength.
The LORD is my rock and my fortress and
    my deliverer;
My God, my strength, in whom I will trust;
My shield and the horn of my salvation,
    my stronghold.
I will call upon the LORD, who is worthy to
    be praised;
So shall I be saved from my enemies.
                                        —*Psalm 18:1–3*

When the LORD brought back the captivity of Zion,
We were like those who dream.
Then our mouth was filled with laughter,
And our tongue with singing.
Then they said among the nations,
"The LORD has done great things for them."
The LORD has done great things for us,
And we are glad.
Bring back our captivity, O LORD,
As the streams in the South.
Those who sow in tears
Shall reap in joy.
He who continually goes forth weeping,
Bearing seed for sowing,
Shall doubtless come again with rejoicing,
Bringing his sheaves with him.

—Psalm 126

The LORD has heard my supplication;
The LORD will receive my prayer.
Let all my enemies be ashamed and greatly troubled;
Let them turn back and be ashamed suddenly.

—Psalm 6:9–11

I will not be afraid of ten thousands of people
Who have set themselves against me all around.

Arise, O Lord;
Save me, O my God!
For You have struck all my enemies on
    the cheekbone;
You have broken the teeth of the ungodly.
—*Psalm 3:6–7*

"Blessed is the Lord God of Israel,
For He has visited and redeemed His people,
And has raised up a horn of salvation for us
In the house of His servant David,
As He spoke by the mouth of His holy prophets,
Who have been since the world began,
That we should be saved from our enemies
And from the hand of all who hate us,
To perform the mercy promised to our fathers
And to remember His holy covenant."
—*Luke 1:68–72*

To You, O LORD, I lift up my soul.
O my God, I trust in You;
Let me not be ashamed;
Let not my enemies triumph over me.
Indeed, let no one who waits on You be ashamed;
Let those be ashamed who deal treacherously
    without cause.
Show me Your ways, O LORD;

Teach me Your paths.
Lead me in Your truth and teach me,
For You are the God of my salvation;
On You I wait all the day

—Psalm 25:1–5

From Fear

The LORD is my light and my salvation;
Whom shall I fear?
The LORD is the strength of my life;
Of whom shall I be afraid?
When the wicked came against me
To eat up my flesh,
My enemies and foes,
They stumbled and fell.
Though an army may encamp against me,
My heart shall not fear;
Though war may rise against me,
In this I will be confident.

—Psalm 27:1–3

There is no fear in love; but perfect love casts out fear, because fear involves torment. But he who fears has not been made perfect in love. We love Him because He first loved us.

—1 John 4:18–19

"When you pass through the waters, I will be
with you;
And through the rivers, they shall not overflow you.

When you walk through the fire, you shall not
    be burned,
Nor shall the flame scorch you."

—Isaiah 43:2

Oh, magnify the LORD with me,
And let us exalt His name together.
I sought the LORD, and He heard me,
And delivered me from all my fears.

—Psalm 34:3–4

The fear of the LORD is the beginning of wisdom;
A good understanding have all those who do
    His commandments.
His praise endures forever.

—Psalm 111:10

Strengthen the weak hands,
And make firm the feeble knees.
Say to those who are fearful-hearted,
"Be strong, do not fear!
Behold, your God will come with vengeance,
With the recompense of God;
He will come and save you."

—Isaiah 35:3–4

God's Wisdom
That Covers You

GOD'S WISDOM THAT COVERS YOU
With His Wings

Your mercy, O LORD, is in the heavens;
Your faithfulness reaches to the clouds.
Your righteousness is like the great mountains;
Your judgments are a great deep;
O LORD, You preserve man and beast.
How precious is Your lovingkindness, O God!
Therefore the children of men put their trust
under the shadow of Your wings.
They are abundantly satisfied with the fullness
    of Your house,
And You give them drink from the river of
    Your pleasures.
For with You is the fountain of life;
In Your light we see light.
Oh, continue Your lovingkindness to those
    who know You,
And Your righteousness to the upright in heart.
—*Psalm 36:5–10*

They utter speech, and speak insolent things;
All the workers of iniquity boast in themselves.
They break in pieces Your people, O LORD,
And afflict Your heritage.
They slay the widow and the stranger,

And murder the fatherless.
Yet they say, "The LORD does not see,
Nor does the God of Jacob understand."
Understand, you senseless among the people;
And you fools, when will you be wise?
He who planted the ear, shall He not hear?
He who formed the eye, shall He not see?
He who instructs the nations, shall He not correct,
He who teaches man knowledge?
The LORD knows the thoughts of man,
That they are futile.

—Psalm 94:4–11

Hear my cry, O God;
Attend to my prayer.
From the end of the earth I will cry to You,
When my heart is overwhelmed;
Lead me to the rock that is higher than I.
For You have been a shelter for me,
A strong tower from the enemy.
I will abide in Your tabernacle forever;
I will trust in the shelter of Your wings.   *Selah*

—Psalm 61:1–4

Uphold my steps in Your paths,
That my footsteps may not slip.
I have called upon You, for You will hear me, O God;

Incline Your ear to me, and hear my speech.
Show Your marvelous lovingkindness by Your
    right hand,
O You who save those who trust in You
From those who rise up against them.
Keep me as the apple of Your eye;
Hide me under the shadow of Your wings,

                         —Psalm 17:5–8

Because You have been my help,
Therefore in the shadow of Your wings I
    will rejoice.
My soul follows close behind You;
Your right hand upholds me.

                         —Psalm 63:7–8

"There is no one like the God of Jeshurun,
Who rides the heavens to help you,
And in His excellency on the clouds.
The eternal God is your refuge,
And underneath are the everlasting arms;
He will thrust out the enemy from before you,
And will say, 'Destroy!'"

               —Deuteronomy 33:26–27

With His Salvation

If you confess with your mouth the Lord Jesus and believe in your heart that God has raised Him from the dead, you will be saved. For with the heart one believes unto righteousness, and with the mouth confession is made unto salvation. For the Scripture says, "Whoever believes on Him will not be put to shame." For there is no distinction between Jew and Greek, for the same Lord over all is rich to all who call upon Him. For "whoever calls on the name of the Lord shall be saved."

—Romans 10:9–13

. . . whom having not seen you love. Though now you do not see Him, yet believing, you rejoice with joy inexpressible and full of glory, receiving the end of your faith—the salvation of your souls. Of this salvation the prophets have inquired and searched carefully, who prophesied of the grace that would come to you.

—1 Peter 1:8–10

. . . not by works of righteousness which we have done, but according to His mercy He saved us, through the washing of regeneration and renewing of the Holy Spirit, whom He poured out on us abundantly through Jesus Christ our Savior.

—*Titus 3:5–6*

For by grace you have been saved through faith, and that not of yourselves; it is the gift of God, not of works, lest anyone should boast. For we are His workmanship, created in Christ Jesus for good works, which God prepared beforehand that we should walk in them.

—*Ephesians 2:8–10*

For God so loved the world that He gave His only begotten Son, that whoever believes in Him should not perish but have everlasting life. For God did not send His Son into the world to condemn the world, but that the world through Him might be saved.

—*John 3:16–17*

Therefore, my beloved, as you have always obeyed, not as in my presence only, but now much more in my absence, work out your own salvation with fear and trembling; for it is God who works in you both to will and to do for His good pleasure.

—*Philippians 2:12–13*

With His Righteousness

This is the message which we have heard from Him and declare to you, that God is light and in Him is no darkness at all. If we say that we have fellowship with Him, and walk in darkness, we lie and do not practice the truth. But if we walk in the light as He is in the light, we have fellowship with one another, and the blood of Jesus Christ His Son cleanses us from all sin. If we say that we have no sin, we deceive ourselves, and the truth is not in us. If we confess our sins, He is faithful and just to forgive us our sins and to cleanse us from all unrighteousness. If we say that we have not sinned, we make Him a liar, and His word is not in us.

—*1 John 1:5–10*

And if Christ is in you, the body is dead because of sin, but the Spirit is life because of righteousness. But if the Spirit of Him who raised Jesus from the dead dwells in you, He who raised Christ from the dead will also give life to your mortal bodies through His Spirit who dwells in you.

—*Romans 8:10–11*

. . . just as Abraham "believed God, and it was accounted to him for righteousness." Therefore know that only those who are of faith are sons of Abraham.

—Galatians 3:6–7

Therefore take up the whole armor of God, that you may be able to withstand in the evil day, and having done all, to stand. Stand therefore, having girded your waist with truth, having put on the breastplate of righteousness, and having shod your feet with the preparation of the gospel of peace; above all, taking the shield of faith with which you will be able to quench all the fiery darts of the wicked one. And take the helmet of salvation, and the sword of the Spirit, which is the word of God.

—Ephesians 6:13–17

A righteous man hates lying,
But a wicked man is loathsome and comes
    to shame.
Righteousness guards him whose way is blameless,
But wickedness overthrows the sinner.

—Proverbs 13:5–6

He who has clean hands and a pure heart,
Who has not lifted up his soul to an idol,

Nor sworn deceitfully.
He shall receive blessing from the LORD,
And righteousness from the God of his salvation.
—*Psalm 24:4–5*

For if by the one man's offense death reigned through the one, much more those who receive abundance of grace and of the gift of righteousness will reign in life through the One, Jesus Christ.
—*Romans 5:17*

GOD'S WISDOM THAT COVERS YOU
With His Presence

Those who trust in the LORD are like Mount Zion,
Which cannot be moved, but abides forever.
As the mountains surround Jerusalem,
So the LORD surrounds His people
From this time forth and forever.

—*Psalm 125:1–2*

What then shall we say to these things? If God is for us, who can be against us? He who did not spare His own Son, but delivered Him up for us all, how shall He not with Him also freely give us all things? Who shall bring a charge against God's elect? It is God who justifies. Who is he who condemns? It is Christ who died, and furthermore is also risen, who is even at the right hand of God, who also makes intercession for us. Who shall separate us from the love of Christ? Shall tribulation, or distress, or persecution, or famine, or nakedness, or peril, or sword? As it is written:

"For Your sake we are killed all day long;

We are accounted as sheep for the slaughter."

Yet in all these things we are more than conquerors through Him who loved us. For I am persuaded that neither death nor life, nor angels nor principalities nor powers, nor things present nor things to come, nor height nor depth, nor any other created thing, shall be able to separate us from the love of God which is in Christ Jesus our Lord.

—*Romans 8:31–39*

"I will give you a new heart and put a new spirit within you; I will take the heart of stone out of your flesh and give you a heart of flesh. I will put My Spirit within you and cause you to walk in My statutes, and you will keep My judgments and do them. Then you shall dwell in the land that I gave to your fathers; you shall be My people, and I will be your God."

—*Ezekiel 36:26–28*

Finally, brethren, farewell. Become complete. Be of good comfort, be of one mind, live in peace; and the God of love and peace will be with you.

—*2 Corinthians 13:11*

Be strong and of good courage, do not fear nor be afraid of them; for the LORD your God, He is the One who goes with you. He will not leave you nor forsake you.

—*Deuteronomy 31:6*

I have set the LORD always before me;
Because He is at my right hand I shall not
   be moved.
Therefore my heart is glad, and my glory rejoices;
My flesh also will rest in hope. . .
You will show me the path of life;
In Your presence is fullness of joy;
At Your right hand are pleasures forevermore.

                   —*Psalm 16:8–9, 11*

GOD'S WISDOM THAT COVERS YOU
With Mercy

O God, my heart is steadfast;
I will sing and give praise, even with my glory.
Awake, lute and harp!
I will awaken the dawn.
I will praise You, O LORD, among the peoples,
And I will sing praises to You among the nations.
For Your mercy is great above the heavens,
And Your truth reaches to the clouds.

—Psalm 108:1–4

I will sing of the mercies of the LORD forever;
With my mouth will I make known Your
    faithfulness to all generations.
For I have said, "Mercy shall be built up forever;
Your faithfulness You shall establish in the
    very heavens."

—Psalm 89:1–2

Many sorrows shall be to the wicked;
But he who trusts in the LORD, mercy shall
    surround him.
Be glad in the LORD and rejoice, you righteous;
And shout for joy, all you upright in heart!

—Psalm 32:10–11

But the mercy of the LORD is from everlasting
    to everlasting
On those who fear Him,
And His righteousness to children's children,
To such as keep His covenant,
And to those who remember His commandments
    to do them.
The LORD has established His throne in heaven,
And His kingdom rules over all.

—Psalm 103:17–19

Our soul waits for the LORD;
He is our help and our shield.
For our heart shall rejoice in Him,
Because we have trusted in His holy name.
Let Your mercy, O LORD, be upon us,
Just as we hope in You.

—Psalm 33:20–22

Enter his gates with thanksgiving
and his courts with praise;
give thanks to him and praise his name.
For the LORD is good and his love endures forever;
his faithfulness continues through all generations.

—Psalm 100:4–5

Be merciful to me, O Lord,
For I cry to You all day long.
Rejoice the soul of Your servant,
For to You, O Lord, I lift up my soul.
For You, Lord, are good, and ready to forgive,
And abundant in mercy to all those who call
  upon You.

—Psalm 86:3–5

God be merciful to us and bless us,
And cause His face to shine upon us, Selah
That Your way may be known on earth,
Your salvation among all nations.

—Psalm 67:1–2

God's Wisdom That
Will Encourage You

Hear my prayer, O LORD,
And let my cry come to You.
Do not hide Your face from me in the day of
    my trouble;
Incline Your ear to me;
In the day that I call, answer me speedily.
For my days are consumed like smoke,
And my bones are burned like a hearth.
My heart is stricken and withered like grass,
So that I forget to eat my bread. . . .
But You, O LORD, shall endure forever,
And the remembrance of Your name to
    all generations.
You will arise and have mercy on Zion;
For the time to favor her,
Yes, the set time, has come

               —Psalm 102:1–4, 12–13

I called on the LORD in distress;
The LORD answered me and set me in a broad place.
The LORD is on my side;
I will not fear.
What can man do to me?

               —Psalm 118:5–6

My flesh and my heart fail;
But God is the strength of my heart and my
    portion forever.
For indeed, those who are far from You shall perish;
You have destroyed all those who desert You
    for harlotry.
But it is good for me to draw near to God;
I have put my trust in the Lord GOD,
That I may declare all Your works.

—Psalm 73:26–28

Hear my cry, O God;
Attend to my prayer.
From the end of the earth I will cry to You,
When my heart is overwhelmed;
Lead me to the rock that is higher than I.
For You have been a shelter for me,
A strong tower from the enemy.

—Psalm 61:1–3

"Ask, and it will be given to you; seek, and you will
find; knock, and it will be opened to you. For everyone who asks receives, and he who seeks finds, and to
him who knocks it will be opened."

—Matthew 7:7–8

"Most assuredly, I say to you, he who believes in Me, the works that I do he will do also; and greater works than these he will do, because I go to My Father. And whatever you ask in My name, that I will do, that the Father may be glorified in the Son. If you ask anything in My name, I will do it."

—*John 14:12–14*

The LORD is near to all who call upon Him,
To all who call upon Him in truth.
He will fulfill the desire of those who fear Him;
He also will hear their cry and save them.
The LORD preserves all who love Him,
But all the wicked He will destroy.

—*Psalm 145:18–20a*

Because you have made the LORD, who is my refuge,
Even the Most High, your dwelling place,
No evil shall befall you,
Nor shall any plague come near your dwelling;
For He shall give His angels charge over you,
To keep you in all your ways. . . .
He shall call upon Me, and I will answer him;
I will be with him in trouble;
I will deliver him and honor him.
With long life I will satisfy him,
And show him My salvation.

—*Psalm 91:9–11, 15–16*

When You Struggle with Doubt

Forever, O LORD,
Your word is settled in heaven.
Your faithfulness endures to all generations;
You established the earth, and it abides.
—*Psalm 119:89–90*

"I will go before you
And make the crooked places straight;
I will break in pieces the gates of bronze
And cut the bars of iron.
I will give you the treasures of darkness
And hidden riches of secret places,
That you may know that I, the LORD,
Who call you by your name,
Am the God of Israel.
For Jacob My servant's sake,
And Israel My elect,
I have even called you by your name;
I have named you, though you have not
    known Me.
I am the LORD, and there is no other;
There is no God besides Me.
I will gird you, though you have not known Me,
That they may know from the rising of the
    sun to its setting

That there is none besides Me.
I am the LORD, and there is no other."

—Isaiah 45:2–6

He will not allow your foot to be moved;
He who keeps you will not slumber.
Behold, He who keeps Israel
Shall neither slumber nor sleep.
The LORD is your keeper;
The LORD is your shade at your right hand.
The sun shall not strike you by day,
Nor the moon by night.
The LORD shall preserve you from all evil;
He shall preserve your soul.

—Psalm 121:3–7

Let my cry come before You, O LORD;
Give me understanding according to Your word.
Let my supplication come before You;
Deliver me according to Your word.

—Psalm 119:169–170

For the Lord GOD will help Me;
Therefore I will not be disgraced;
Therefore I have set My face like a flint,
And I know that I will not be ashamed. . . .

Who among you fears the LORD?
Who obeys the voice of His Servant?
Who walks in darkness
And has no light?
Let him trust in the name of the LORD
And rely upon his God.

—Isaiah 50:7, 10

"Let not your heart be troubled; you believe in God, believe also in Me. In My Father's house are many mansions; if it were not so, I would have told you. I go to prepare a place for you. And if I go and prepare a place for you, I will come again and receive you to Myself; that where I am, there you may be also."

—John 14:1–3

"Peace I leave with you, My peace I give to you; not as the world gives do I give to you. Let not your heart be troubled, neither let it be afraid. You have heard Me say to you, 'I am going away and coming back to you.' If you loved Me, you would rejoice because I said, 'I am going to the Father,' for My Father is greater than I. And now I have told you before it comes, that when it does come to pass, you may believe."

—John 14:27–29

For I am not ashamed of the gospel of Christ, for it is the power of God to salvation for everyone who believes, for the Jew first and also for the Greek. For in it the righteousness of God is revealed from faith to faith; as it is written, "The just shall live by faith."

For the wrath of God is revealed from heaven against all ungodliness and unrighteousness of men, who suppress the truth in unrighteousness, because what may be known of God is manifest in them, for God has shown it to them. For since the creation of the world His invisible attributes are clearly seen, being understood by the things that are made, even His eternal power and Godhead, so that they are without excuse.

—Romans 1:16–20

Now to Him who is able to keep you from
    stumbling,
And to present you faultless
Before the presence of His glory with exceeding joy,
To God our Savior,
Who alone is wise,
Be glory and majesty,
Dominion and power,
Both now and forever.
Amen.

—Jude 24–25

When a Loved One Dies

And since we have the same spirit of faith, according to what is written, "I believed and therefore I spoke," we also believe and therefore speak, knowing that He who raised up the Lord Jesus will also raise us up with Jesus, and will present us with you.

—*2 Corinthians 4:13–14*

The pains of death surrounded me,
And the pangs of Sheol laid hold of me;
I found trouble and sorrow.
Then I called upon the name of the LORD:
"O LORD, I implore You, deliver my soul!"
Gracious is the LORD, and righteous;
Yes, our God is merciful.

—*Psalm 116:3–5*

Into Your hand I commit my spirit;
You have redeemed me, O LORD God of truth. . . .
I will be glad and rejoice in Your mercy,
For You have considered my trouble;
You have known my soul in adversities,
And have not shut me up into the hand of
    the enemy;

You have set my feet in a wide place.
Have mercy on me, O Lord, for I am in trouble;
My eye wastes away with grief,
Yes, my soul and my body! . . .
But as for me, I trust in You, O Lord;
I say, "You are my God."

—*Psalm 31:5, 7–9, 14*

But now Christ is risen from the dead, and has become the firstfruits of those who have fallen asleep. For since by man came death, by Man also came the resurrection of the dead. For as in Adam all die, even so in Christ all shall be made alive. But each one in his own order: Christ the firstfruits, afterward those who are Christ's at His coming. Then comes the end, when He delivers the kingdom to God the Father, when He puts an end to all rule and all authority and power. For He must reign till He has put all enemies under His feet. The last enemy that will be destroyed is death. For "He has put all things under His feet." But when He says "all things are put under Him," it is evident that He who put all things under Him is excepted. Now when all things are made subject to Him, then the Son Himself will also be subject to Him who put all things under Him, that God may be all in all.

—*1 Corinthians 15:20–28*

Behold, I tell you a mystery: We shall not all sleep, but we shall all be changed—in a moment, in the twinkling of an eye, at the last trumpet. For the trumpet will sound, and the dead will be raised incorruptible, and we shall be changed. For this corruptible must put on incorruption, and this mortal must put on immortality. So when this corruptible has put on incorruption, and this mortal has put on immortality, then shall be brought to pass the saying that is written: "Death is swallowed up in victory."

"O Death, where is your sting?

O Hades, where is your victory?"

The sting of death is sin, and the strength of sin is the law. But thanks be to God, who gives us the victory through our Lord Jesus Christ.

—1 Corinthians 15:51–57

When You Know Persecution

Save me, O God, by Your name,
And vindicate me by Your strength.
Hear my prayer, O God;
Give ear to the words of my mouth.
For strangers have risen up against me,
And oppressors have sought after my life;
They have not set God before them. Selah
Behold, God is my helper;
The Lord is with those who uphold my life.
He will repay my enemies for their evil.
Cut them off in Your truth.
I will freely sacrifice to You;
I will praise Your name, O LORD, for it is good.
For He has delivered me out of all trouble;
And my eye has seen its desire upon my enemies.

—*Psalm 54:1–7*

Be merciful to me, O God, be merciful to me!
For my soul trusts in You;
And in the shadow of Your wings I will make
    my refuge,
Until these calamities have passed by.
I will cry out to God Most High,
To God who performs all things for me.

He shall send from heaven and save me;
He reproaches the one who would swallow me up.

Selah

God shall send forth His mercy and His truth.
My soul is among lions;
I lie among the sons of men
Who are set on fire,
Whose teeth are spears and arrows,
And their tongue a sharp sword.
Be exalted, O God, above the heavens;
Let Your glory be above all the earth.

—*Psalm 57:1–5*

"If the world hates you, you know that it hated Me before it hated you. If you were of the world, the world would love its own. Yet because you are not of the world, but I chose you out of the world, therefore the world hates you. Remember the word that I said to you, 'A servant is not greater than his master.' If they persecuted Me, they will also persecute you. If they kept My word, they will keep yours also. But all these things they will do to you for My name's sake, because they do not know Him who sent Me."

—*John 15:18–21*

But you, beloved, remember the words which were spoken before by the apostles of our Lord Jesus

Christ: how they told you that there would be mockers in the last time who would walk according to their own ungodly lusts. These are sensual persons, who cause divisions, not having the Spirit.

But you, beloved, building yourselves up on your most holy faith, praying in the Holy Spirit, keep yourselves in the love of God, looking for the mercy of our Lord Jesus Christ unto eternal life.

—*Jude 17–21*

But we have this treasure in earthen vessels, that the excellence of the power may be of God and not of us. We are hard-pressed on every side, yet not crushed; we are perplexed, but not in despair; persecuted, but not forsaken; struck down, but not destroyed—always carrying about in the body the dying of the Lord Jesus, that the life of Jesus also may be manifested in our body. For we who live are always delivered to death for Jesus' sake, that the life of Jesus also may be manifested in our mortal flesh.

—*2 Corinthians 4:7–11*

When You are Weary

Have mercy on me, O LORD, for I am weak;
O LORD, heal me, for my bones are troubled.
My soul also is greatly troubled;
But You, O LORD —how long?
Return, O LORD, deliver me!
Oh, save me for Your mercies' sake!
For in death there is no remembrance of You;
In the grave who will give You thanks?
I am weary with my groaning;
All night I make my bed swim;
I drench my couch with my tears.
My eye wastes away because of grief;
It grows old because of all my enemies.
Depart from me, all you workers of iniquity;
For the Lord has heard the voice of my weeping.
    —*Psalm 6:2–8*

Have you not known?
Have you not heard?
The everlasting God, the LORD,
The Creator of the ends of the earth,
Neither faints nor is weary.
His understanding is unsearchable.
He gives power to the weak,

And to those who have no might He
    increases strength.
Even the youths shall faint and be weary,
And the young men shall utterly fall,
But those who wait on the LORD
Shall renew their strength;
They shall mount up with wings like eagles,
They shall run and not be weary,
They shall walk and not faint.

—Isaiah 40:28–31

For all things are for your sakes, that grace, having spread through the many, may cause thanksgiving to abound to the glory of God.

Therefore we do not lose heart. Even though our outward man is perishing, yet the inward man is being renewed day by day. For our light affliction, which is but for a moment, is working for us a far more exceeding and eternal weight of glory, while we do not look at the things which are seen, but at the things which are not seen. For the things which are seen are temporary, but the things which are not seen are eternal.

—2 Corinthians 4:15–18

Do not be deceived, God is not mocked; for whatever a man sows, that he will also reap. For he who sows to his flesh will of the flesh reap corruption, but he who sows to the Spirit will of the Spirit reap everlasting life. And let us not grow weary while doing good, for in due season we shall reap if we do not lose heart. Therefore, as we have opportunity, let us do good to all, especially to those who are of the household of faith.

—*Galatians 6:7–10*

"And whatever you ask in My name, that I will do, that the Father may be glorified in the Son. If you ask anything in My name, I will do it. If you love Me, keep My commandments. And I will pray the Father, and He will give you another Helper, that He may abide with you forever—the Spirit of truth, whom the world cannot receive, because it neither sees Him nor knows Him; but you know Him, for He dwells with you and will be in you. I will not leave you orphans; I will come to you."

—*John 14:13–18*

You will keep him in perfect peace,
Whose mind is stayed on You,
Because he trusts in You.
Trust in the LORD forever,
For in YAH, the LORD, is everlasting strength.

—*Isaiah 26:3–4*

Teach me, O LORD, the way of Your statutes,
And I shall keep it to the end.
Give me understanding, and I shall keep Your law;
Indeed, I shall observe it with my whole heart.
Make me walk in the path of Your commandments,
For I delight in it.
Incline my heart to Your testimonies,
And not to covetousness.
Turn away my eyes from looking at worthless things,
And revive me in Your way.

—Psalm 119:33–37

When You Feel Alone

You are my hiding place;
You shall preserve me from trouble;
You shall surround me with songs of deliverance.

Selah

I will instruct you and teach you in the way you
    should go;
I will guide you with My eye.

—*Psalm 32:7–8*

But as for me, my prayer is to You,
O LORD, in the acceptable time;
O God, in the multitude of Your mercy,
Hear me in the truth of Your salvation.
Deliver me out of the mire,
And let me not sink;
Let me be delivered from those who hate me,
And out of the deep waters.
Let not the floodwater overflow me,
Nor let the deep swallow me up;
And let not the pit shut its mouth on me.
Hear me, O LORD, for Your lovingkindness is good;
Turn to me according to the multitude of Your
    tender mercies.
And do not hide Your face from Your servant,

For I am in trouble;
Hear me speedily.
Draw near to my soul, and redeem it;
Deliver me because of my enemies.

—Psalm 69:13–18a

And you He made alive, who were dead in trespasses and sins, in which you once walked according to the course of this world, according to the prince of the power of the air, the spirit who now works in the sons of disobedience, among whom also we all once conducted ourselves in the lusts of our flesh, fulfilling the desires of the flesh and of the mind, and were by nature children of wrath, just as the others. But God, who is rich in mercy, because of His great love with which He loved us, even when we were dead in trespasses, made us alive together with Christ (by grace you have been saved).

—Ephesians 2:1–5

I wait for the Lord, my soul waits,
And in His word I do hope.
My soul waits for the Lord
More than those who watch for the morning—
Yes, more than those who watch for
    the morning.
O Israel, hope in the Lord;

For with the LORD there is mercy,
And with Him is abundant redemption.

—*Psalm 130:5–7*

You are my portion, O LORD;
I have said that I would keep Your words.
I entreated Your favor with my whole heart;
Be merciful to me according to Your word.
I thought about my ways,
And turned my feet to Your testimonies.
I made haste, and did not delay
To keep Your commandments. . . .
I am a companion of all who fear You,
And of those who keep Your precepts.
The earth, O LORD, is full of Your mercy;
Teach me Your statutes.

—*Psalm 119:57–60, 63–64*

When a Loved One Rejects God

And you He made alive, who were dead in trespasses and sins, in which you once walked according to the course of this world, according to the prince of the power of the air, the spirit who now works in the sons of disobedience, among whom also we all once conducted ourselves in the lusts of our flesh, fulfilling the desires of the flesh and of the mind, and were by nature children of wrath, just as the others. But God, who is rich in mercy, because of His great love with which He loved us, even when we were dead in trespasses, made us alive together with Christ (by grace you have been saved).

—*Ephesians 2:1–5*

Say to those who are fearful-hearted,
"Be strong, do not fear!
Behold, your God will come with vengeance,
With the recompense of God;
He will come and save you."
Then the eyes of the blind shall be opened,
And the ears of the deaf shall be unstopped.

—*Isaiah 35:4–5*

Then You spoke in a vision to Your holy one,
And said: "I have given help to one who is mighty;
I have exalted one chosen from the people. . . .
"If his sons forsake My law
And do not walk in My judgments,
If they break My statutes
And do not keep My commandments,
Then I will punish their transgression with the rod,
And their iniquity with stripes.
Nevertheless My lovingkindness I will not utterly
   take from him,
Nor allow My faithfulness to fail.
My covenant I will not break,
Nor alter the word that has gone out of My lips."
—*Psalm 89:19, 30–34*

And Jesus said to him, "Today salvation has come
to this house, because he also is a son of Abraham;
for the Son of Man has come to seek and to save that
which was lost."
—*Luke 19:9–10*

I wait for the LORD, my soul waits,
And in His word I do hope.
My soul waits for the Lord
More than those who watch for the morning—
Yes, more than those who watch for the morning.

O Israel, hope in the LORD;
For with the LORD there is mercy,
And with Him is abundant redemption.

—*Psalm 130:5–7*

"Yet hear me now, O Jacob My servant,
And Israel whom I have chosen.
Thus says the LORD who made you
And formed you from the womb, who will
    help you:
'Fear not, O Jacob My servant;
And you, Jeshurun, whom I have chosen.
For I will pour water on him who is thirsty,
And floods on the dry ground;
I will pour My Spirit on your descendants,
And My blessing on your offspring;
They will spring up among the grass
Like willows by the watercourses.'
One will say, 'I am the LORD's';
Another will call himself by the name of Jacob;
Another will write with his hand, 'The LORD's,'
And name himself by the name of Israel.
"Thus says the LORD, the King of Israel,
And his Redeemer, the LORD of hosts:
'I am the First and I am the Last;
Besides Me there is no God.
And who can proclaim as I do?
Then let him declare it and set it in order for Me,

Since I appointed the ancient people.
And the things that are coming and shall come,
Let them show these to them.'"

—Isaiah 44:1–7

Prayer List

Prayer List

Prayer List

Prayer List

Prayer List

Prayer List

Personal Study Notes

Personal Study Notes

Personal Study Notes

Personal Study Notes

Personal Study Notes

Personal Study Notes

Personal Study Notes